Serenity

an

Adult Coloring Book

by Kiersten Fay

Color Mandalas for Tranquility and Relaxation

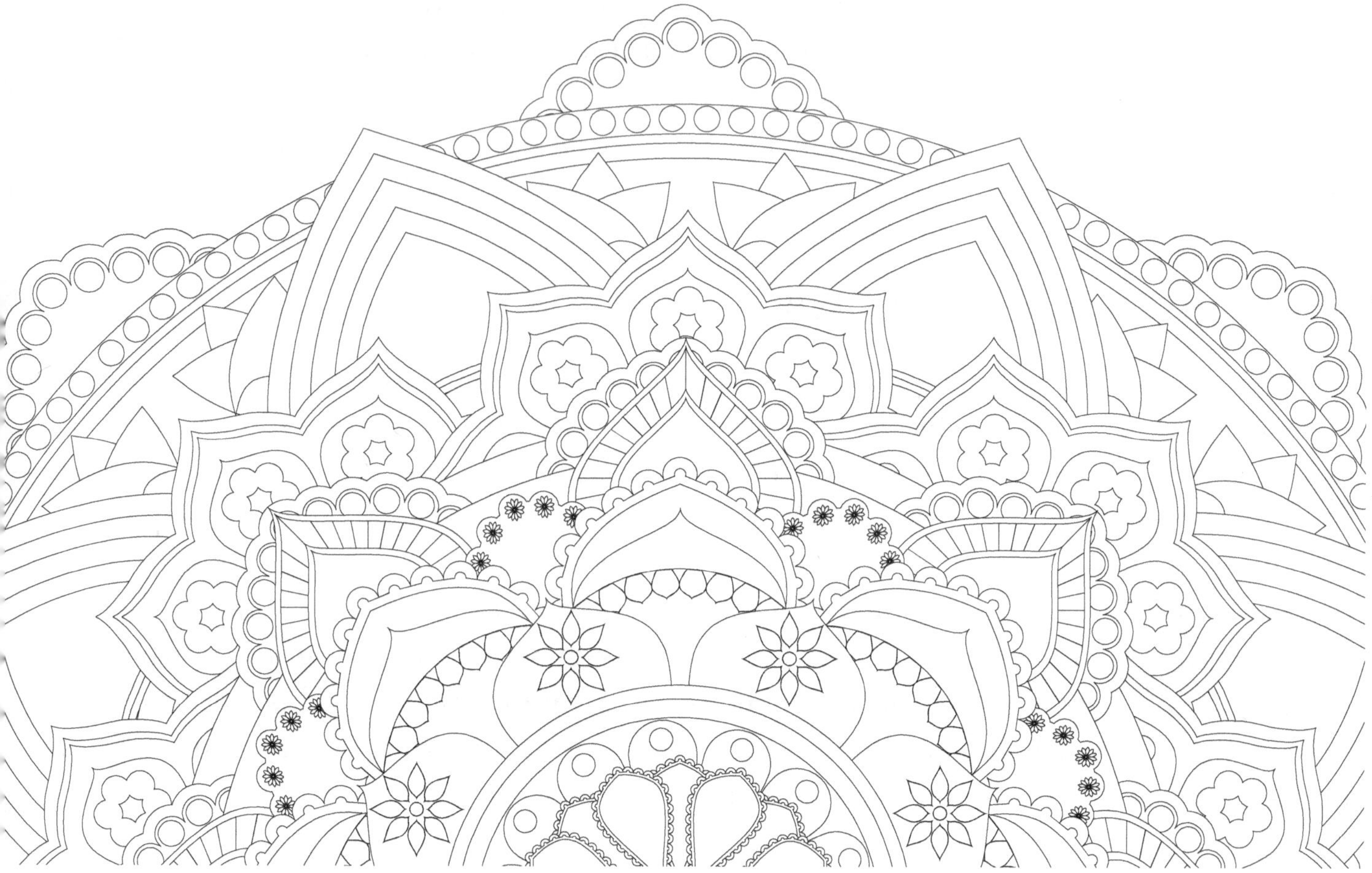

Why should I color?

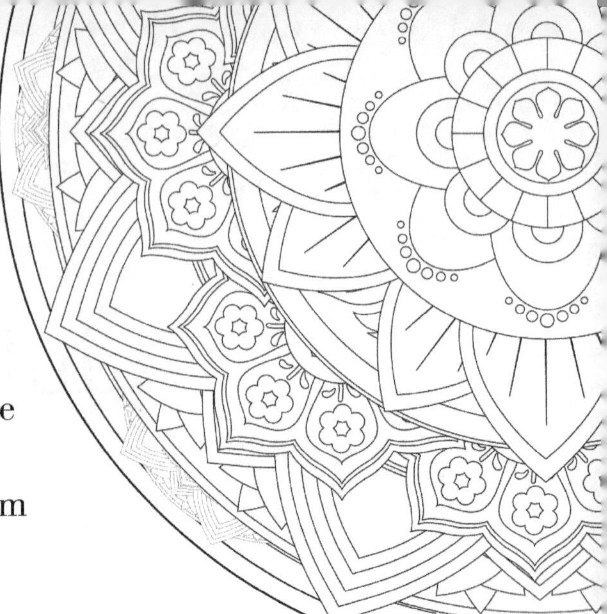

❀ According to researchers at Johns Hopkins University and the editors of Yoga Journal, coloring can be a form of meditation. Why is meditation a healthy pursuit? Well, studies have shown that meditation not only lowers blood pressure but can also boost your immune system while improving your ability to concentrate.

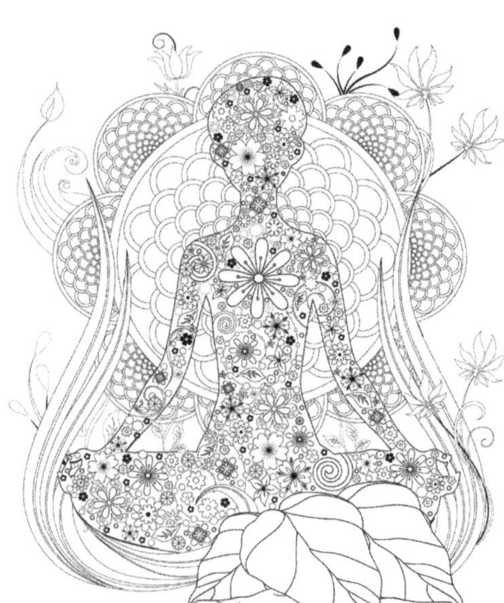

❀ The key in most cases is stress.

We live in a fast-paced world, bombarded by electronics such as smart phones, apps, television, computers, and the Internet. Add that to the daily grind, work, and family obligations, and by the end of the day we are exhausted mentally, stressed out, and physically weary. For those who find it difficult to reach that coveted zen-like state and clear our minds through meditation, or even just have a hard time relaxing, an activity such as coloring can work wonders.

❀ From my personal experience:

In 1995 I worked in technical support for an Internet company. Anyone remember Prodigy Internet? No? Well anyway, like most writers I am fairly introverted–even more so back then. Speaking with people, even over the phone, while they are angry about their current Internet malfunction, was very stressful for me. One day I had some colored gel pens with me and started doodling while troubleshooting calls. Before I knew it, my simple notebook paper was filled with a glorious mountain scene decorated by evergreens that framed a tranquil river...and my shift was over. And I felt good! The next day, I grabbed whatever coloring books I could find, a pack of pencils, pens, and markers, and brought them to work with me. It really helped to relieve the stress of my job. And, with an inner grin, I'd noticed several others around me were following my example.

Some of the intricate designs you'll find throughout this book.

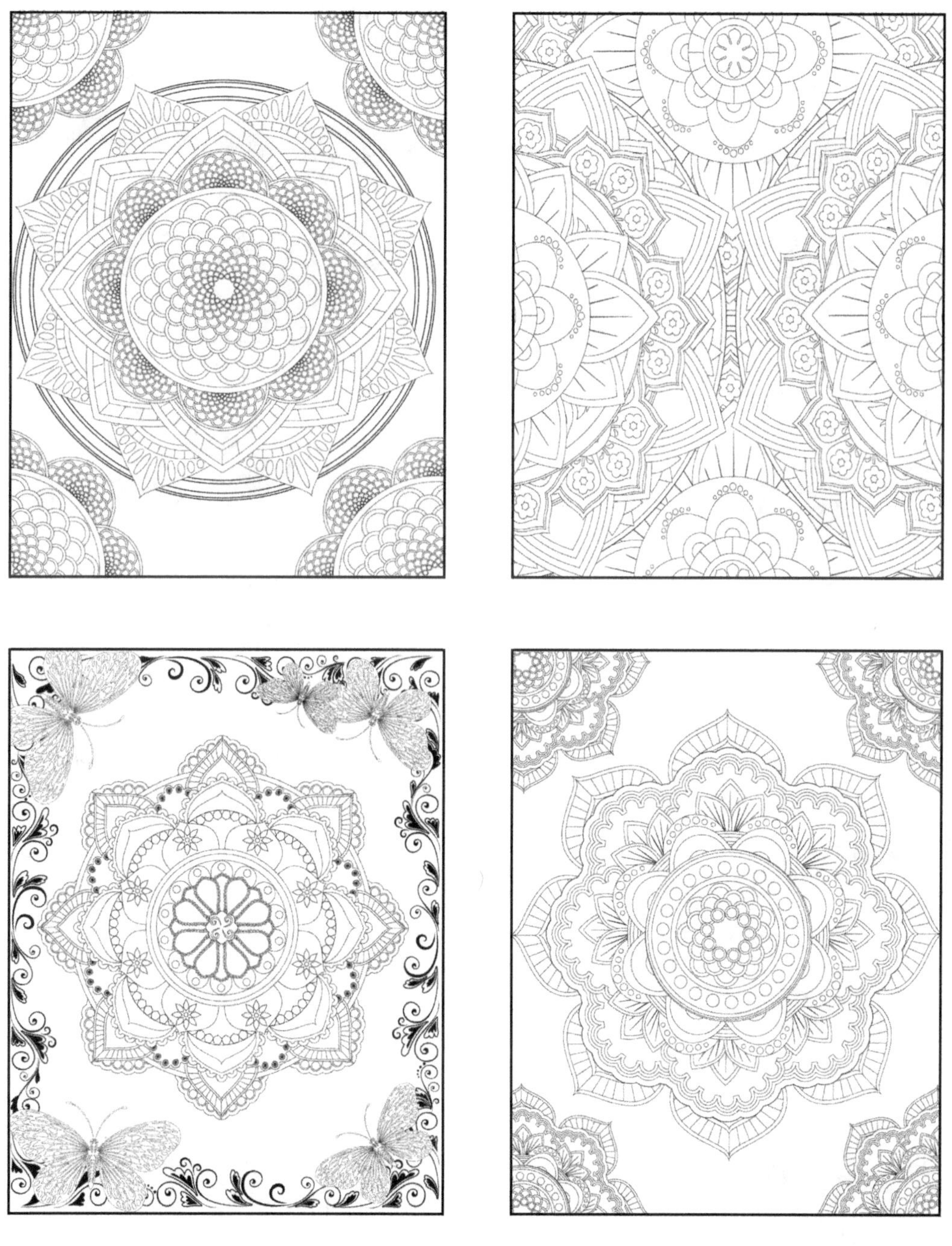

Coloring Tips

Coloring can be as simple or as complicated as you want it to be. Incorporate shading and blending techniques for a dynamic look, or merely lose yourself in coloring inside the lines. Crayons are okay, but colored pencils are where it's at. Get yourself a large set and go to town.

Shading: find two colors that blend well together. Use the dark for the shadow and the lighter color as the highlight.

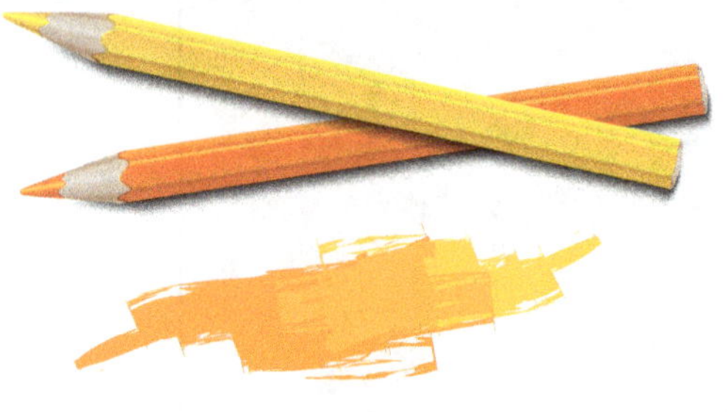

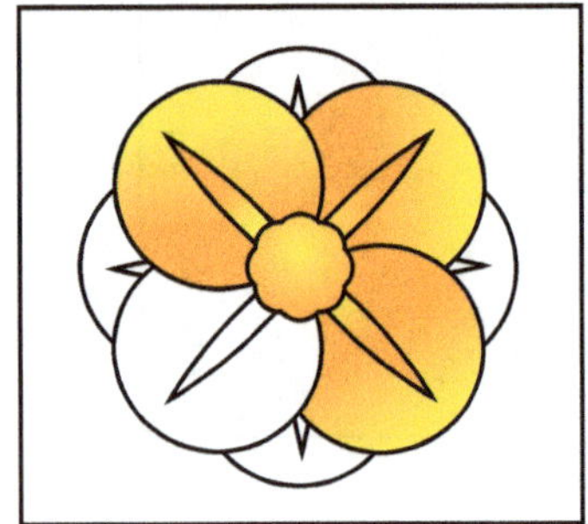

Stippling and hatching: use lines or dots instead of filling in the whole area with a solid color. The results are amazing.

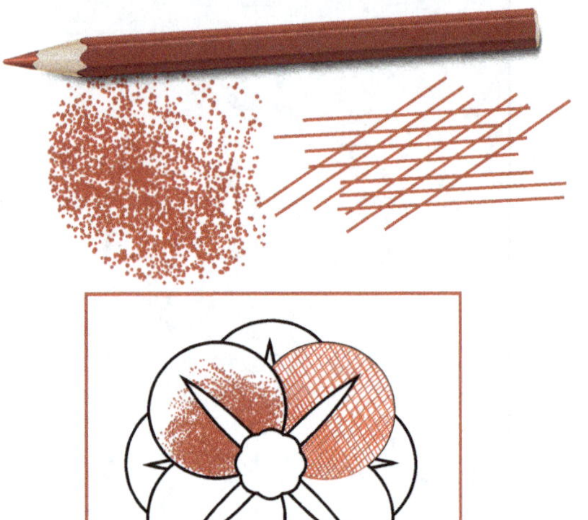

Outlining: Use one color to outline and another to fill in the area.

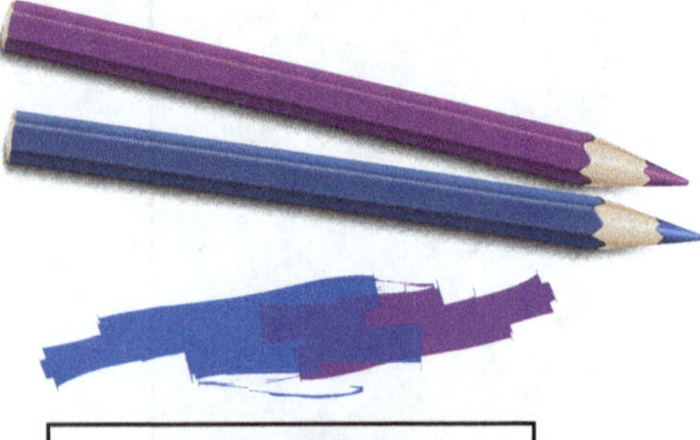

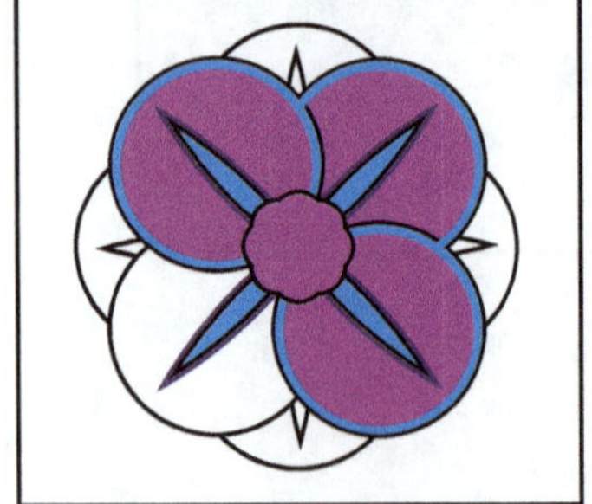

Pressure: Using one color, press hard for a darker look and then lighten the pressure for a smooth gradient appearance.

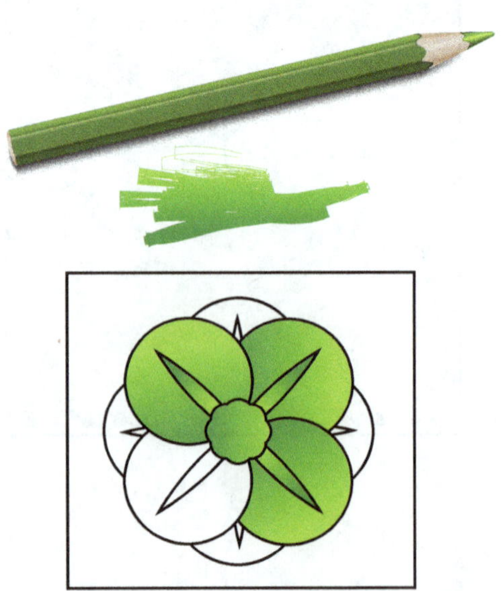

Color Wheel

The color wheel is nearly as old as art itself and has been utilized by countless artists. The colors opposite each other on the wheel are called complimentary colors, and can offer a sense of drama or vibrancy when used together. Analogous colors (colors directly next to each other) are often used to create serene and comforting designs.

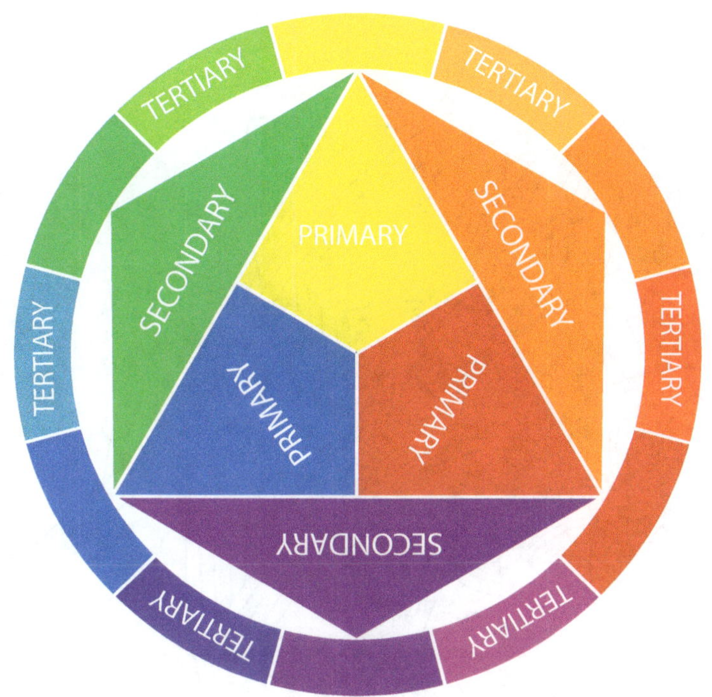

Primary Colors: Red, yellow, and blue. These are the three primary colors that cannot be created by any combination of other colors. All other colors are derived from these three hues.

Secondary Colors: Green, orange, and purple. These are the colors formed by mixing two primary colors.

Tertiary Colors: Yellow-orange, red-orange, red-purple, blue-purple, blue-green, and yellow-green. These are the colors formed by mixing a primary and a secondary color. That's why they have two word names, such as blue-green, red-violet, and yellow-orange.

Share Your Creations!

Once you start coloring, the page becomes your artistic expression, something unique to the world, and we want to see it! Come to our Facebook page and share your creations with us.

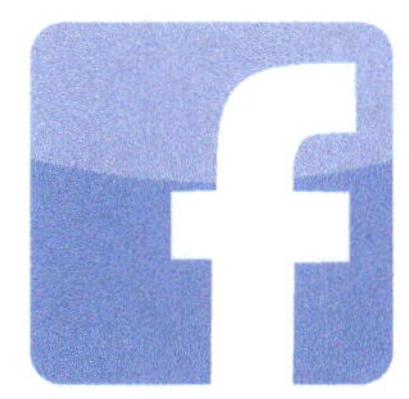

www.Facebook.com/AdultsColoringForFun

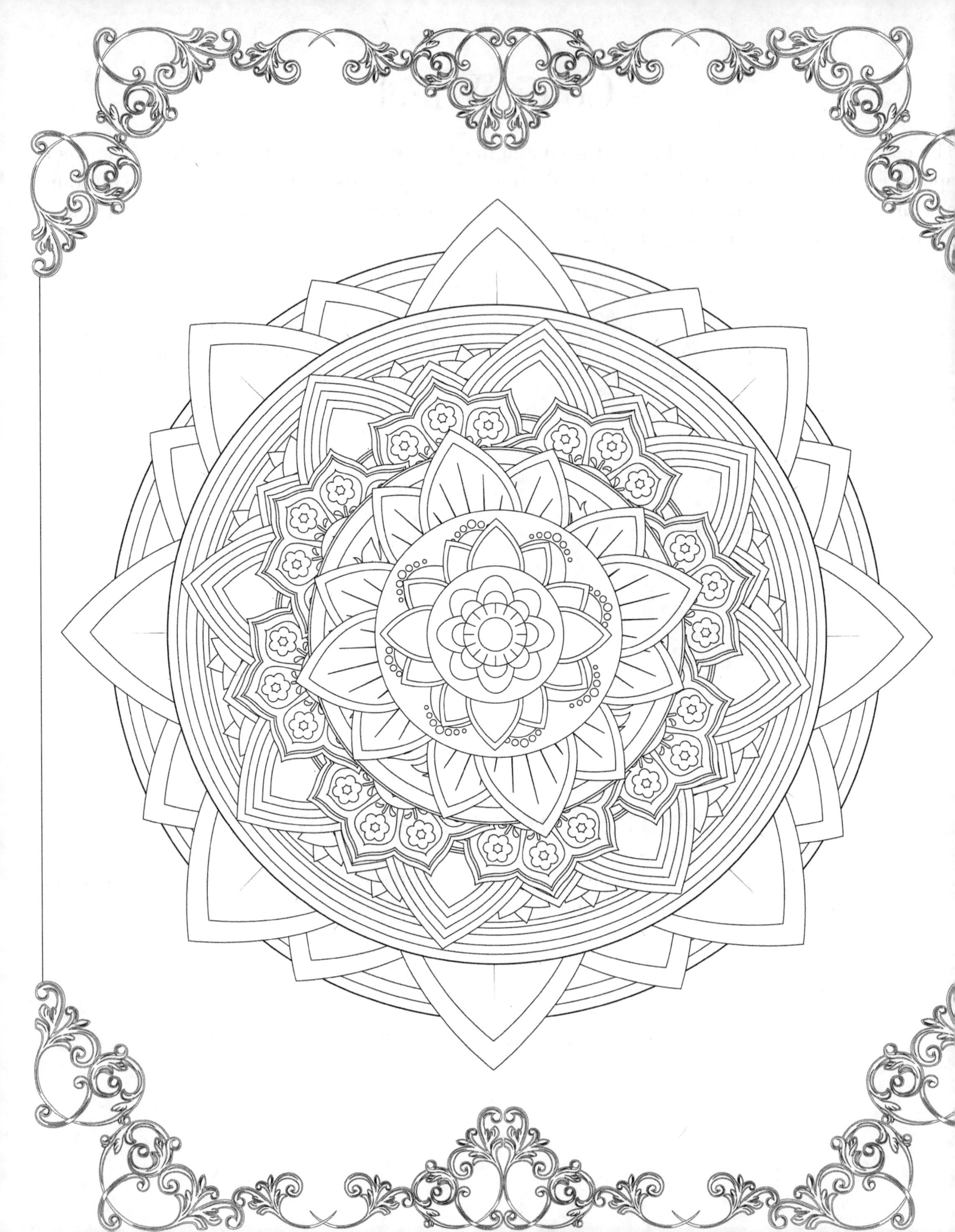

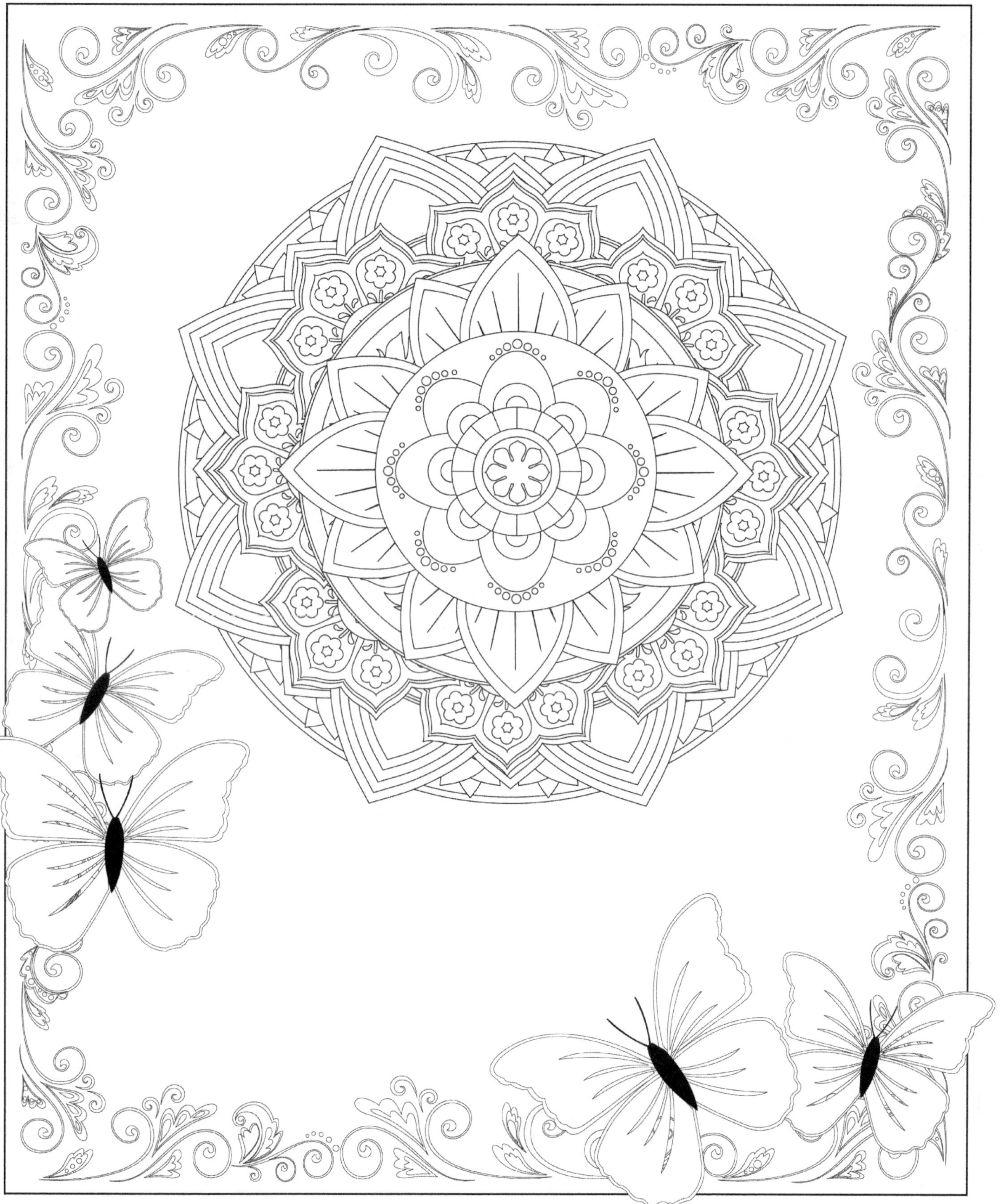

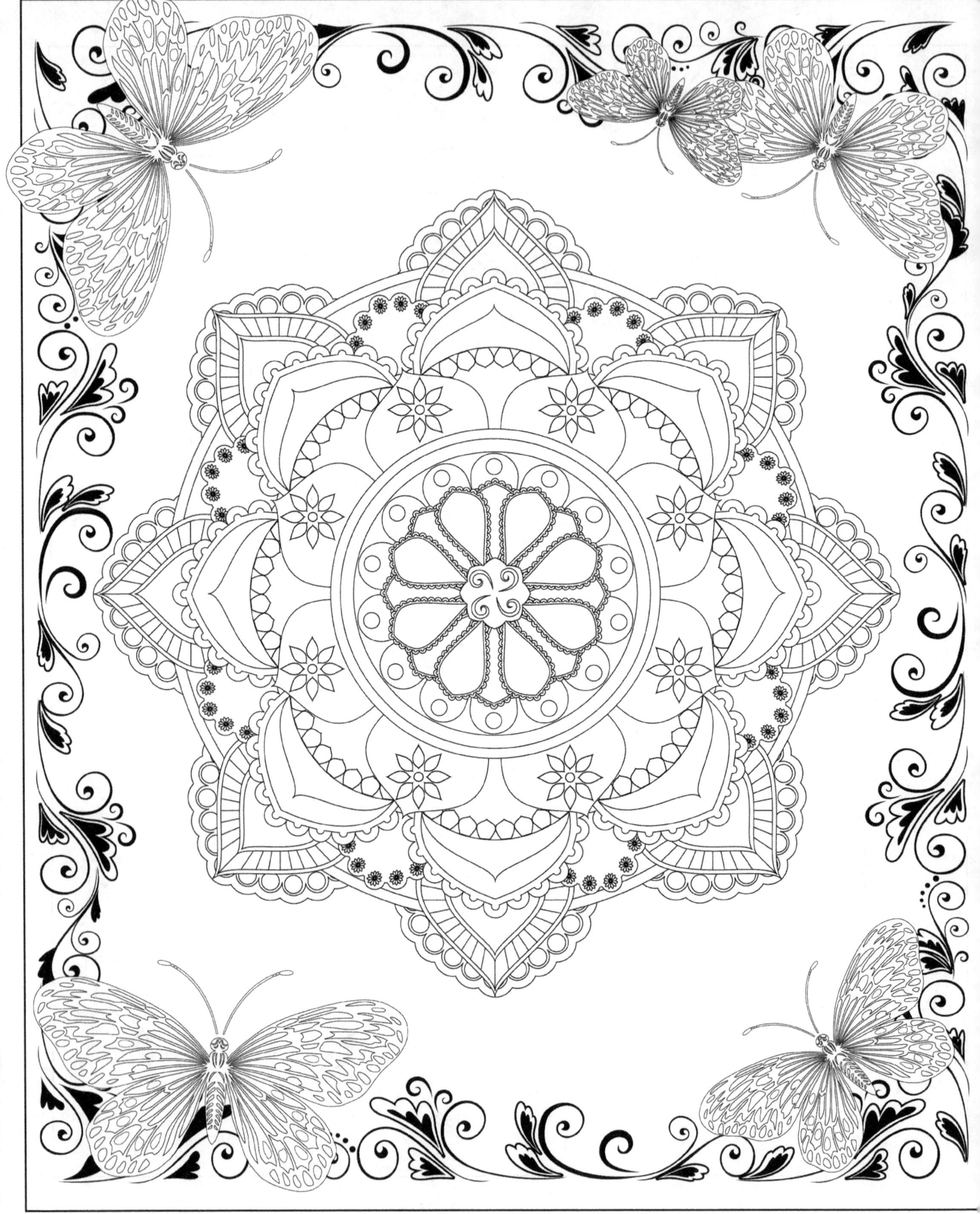

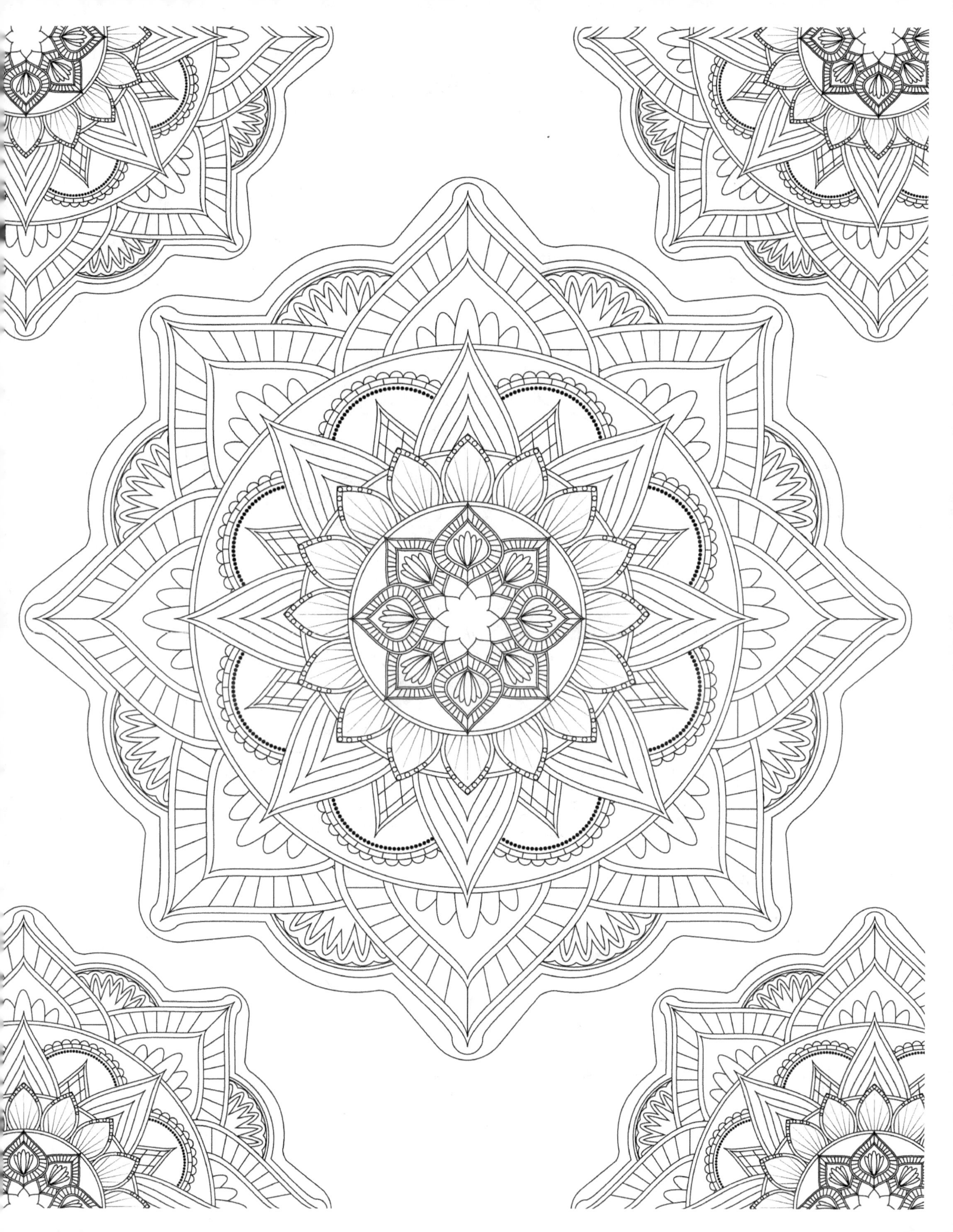

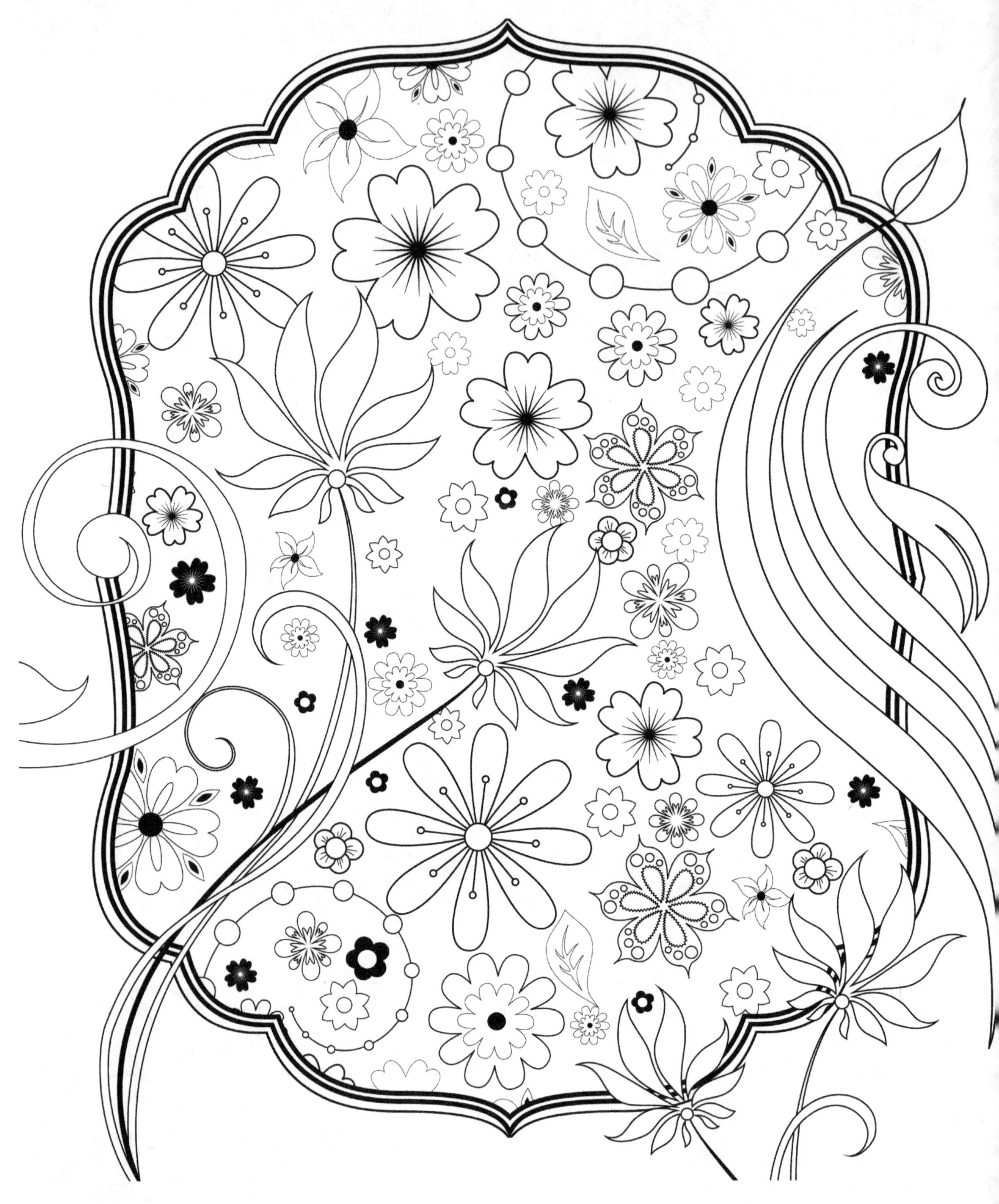

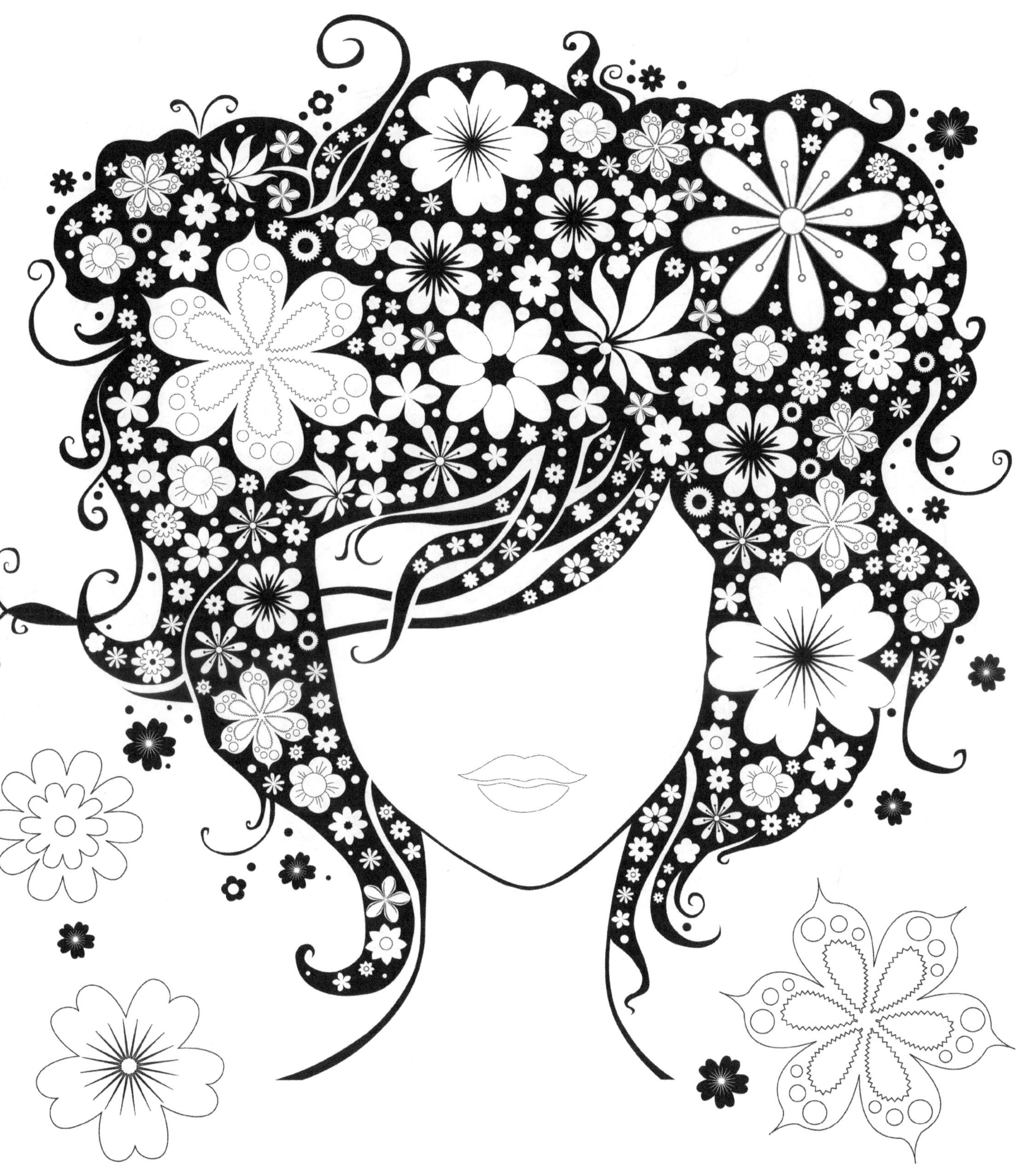

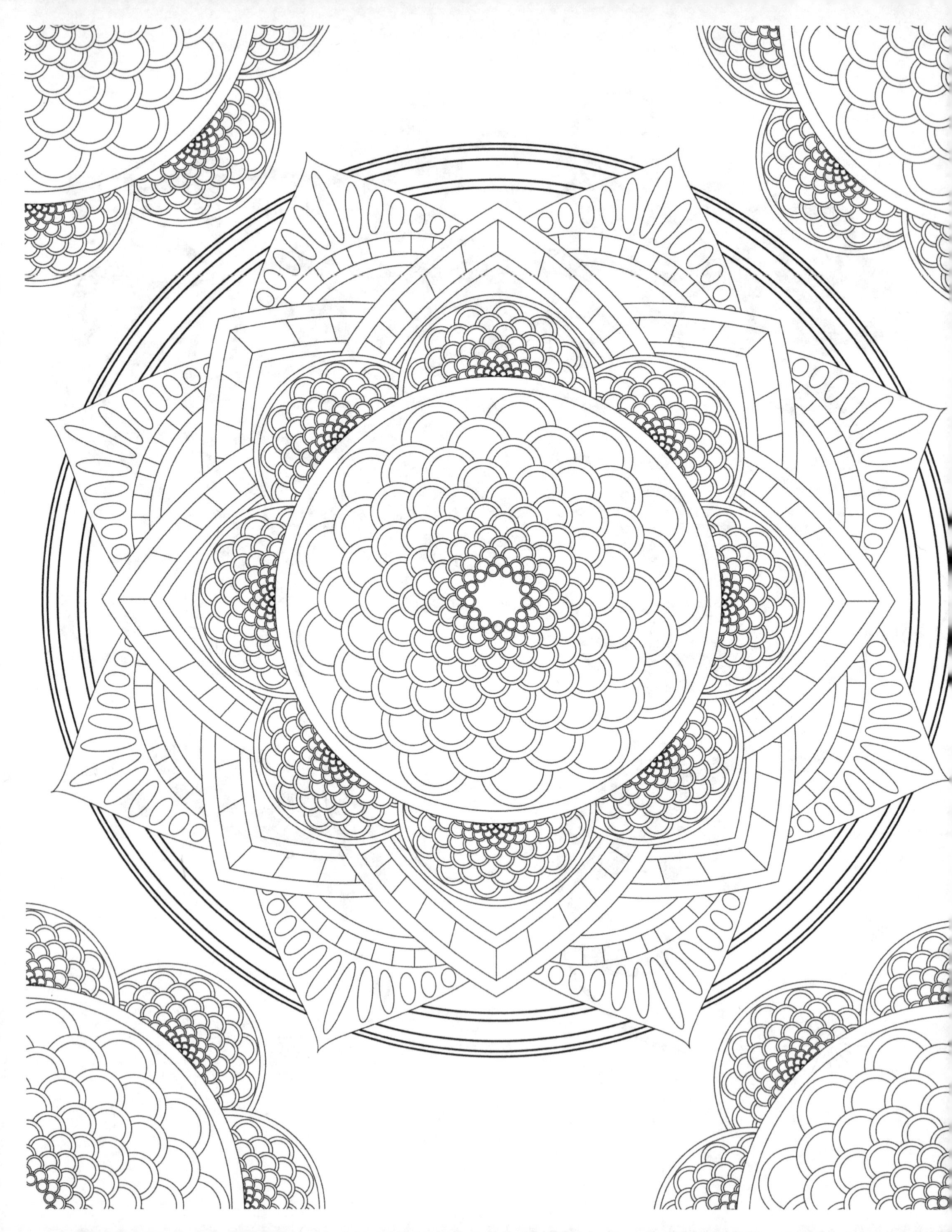

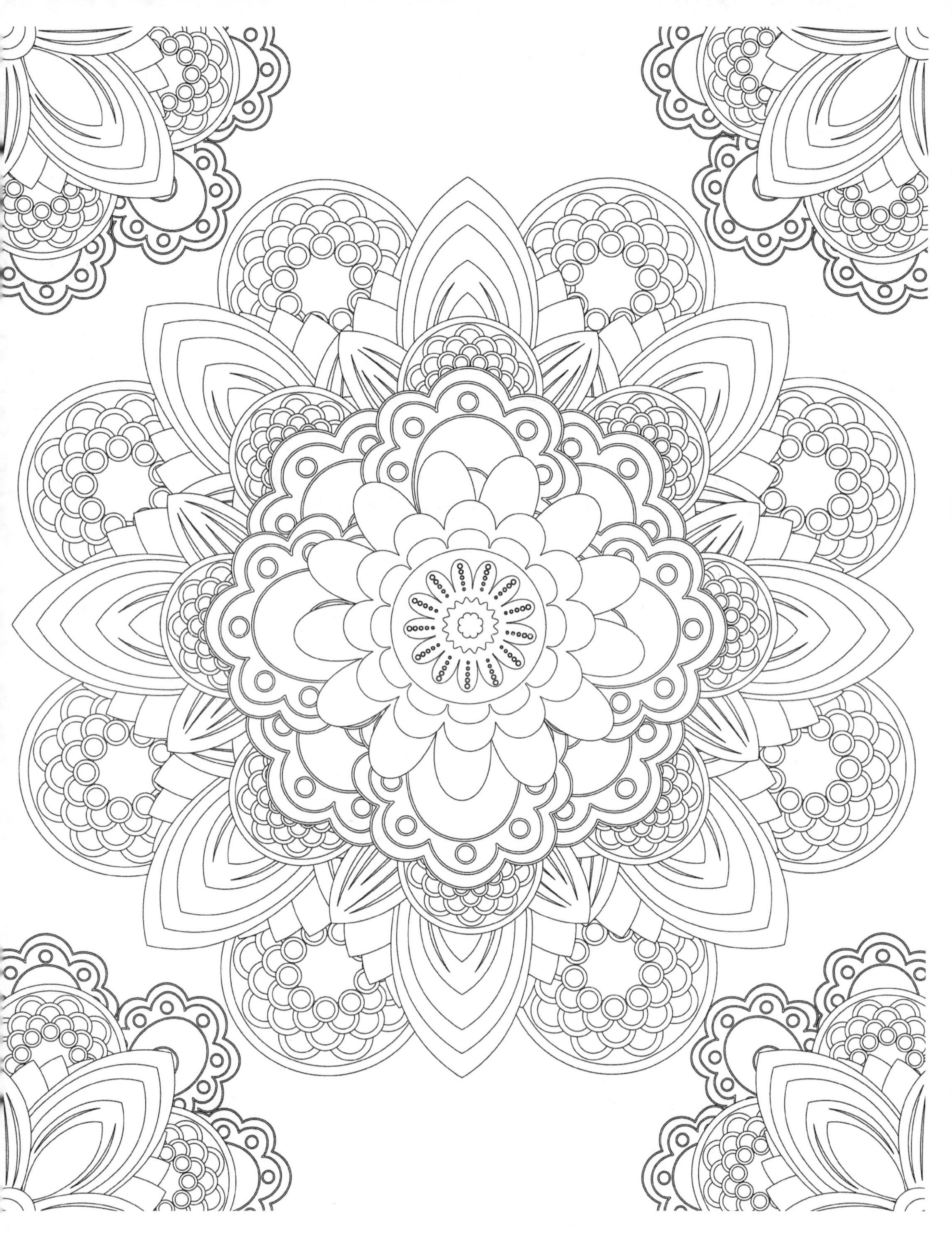

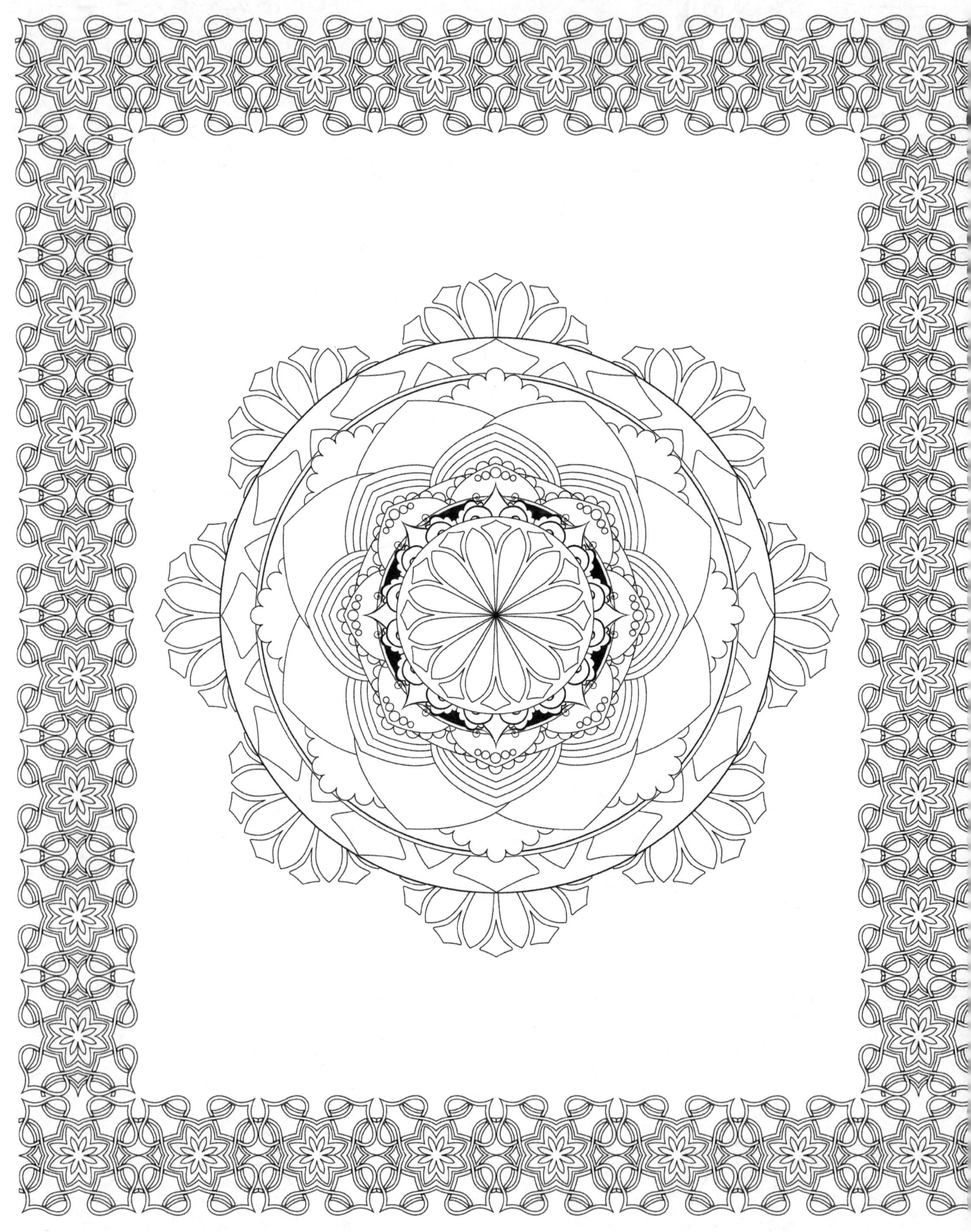

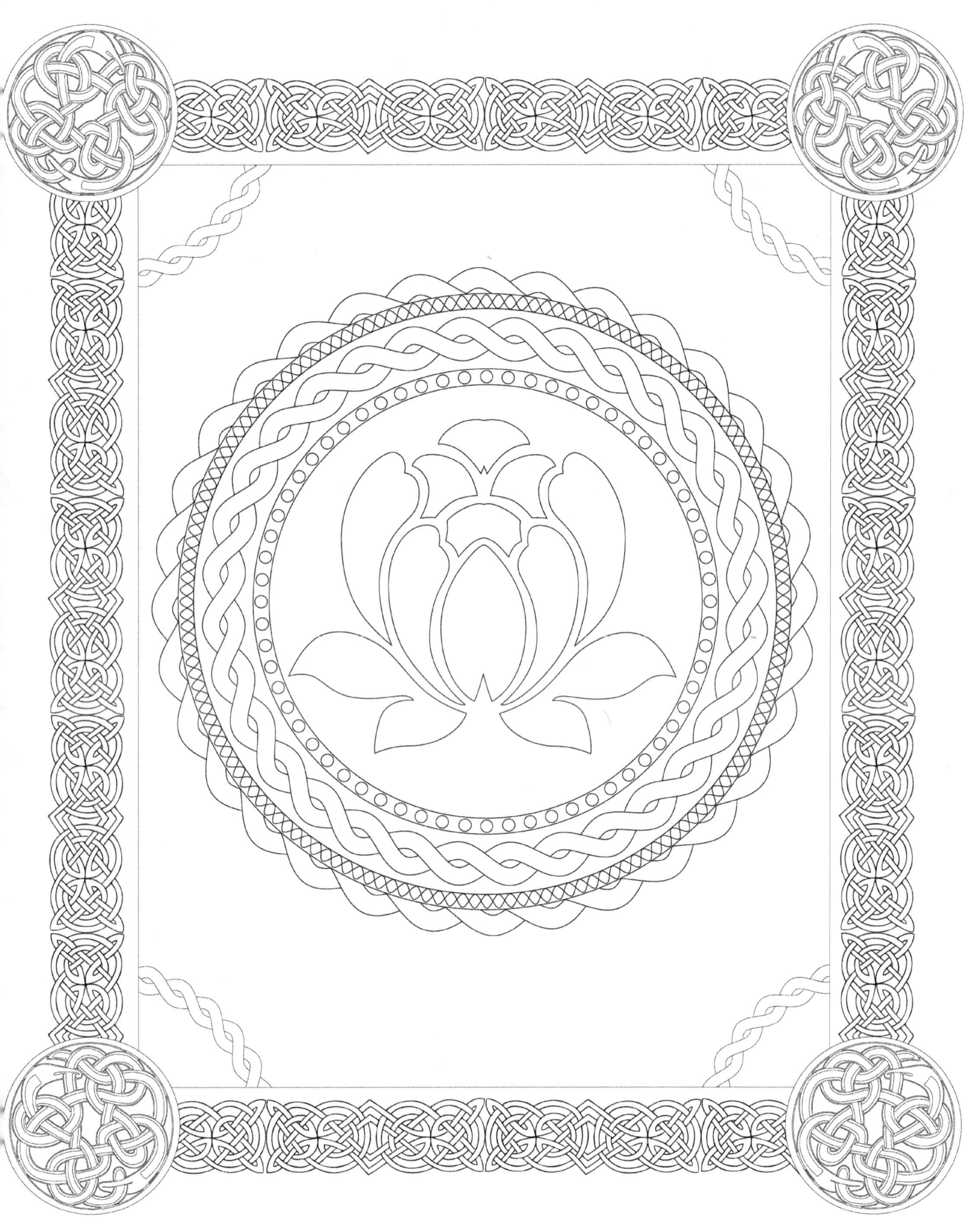

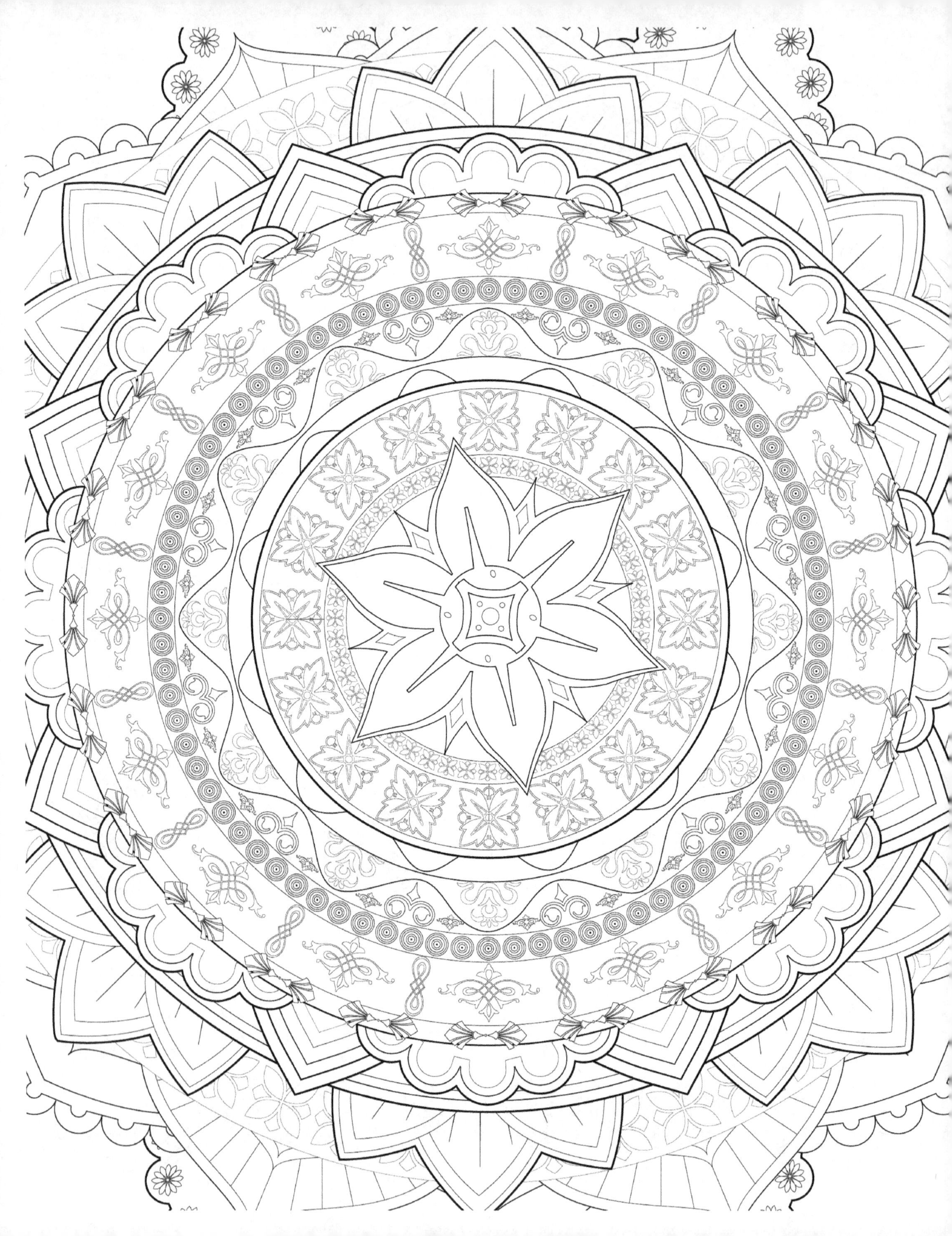

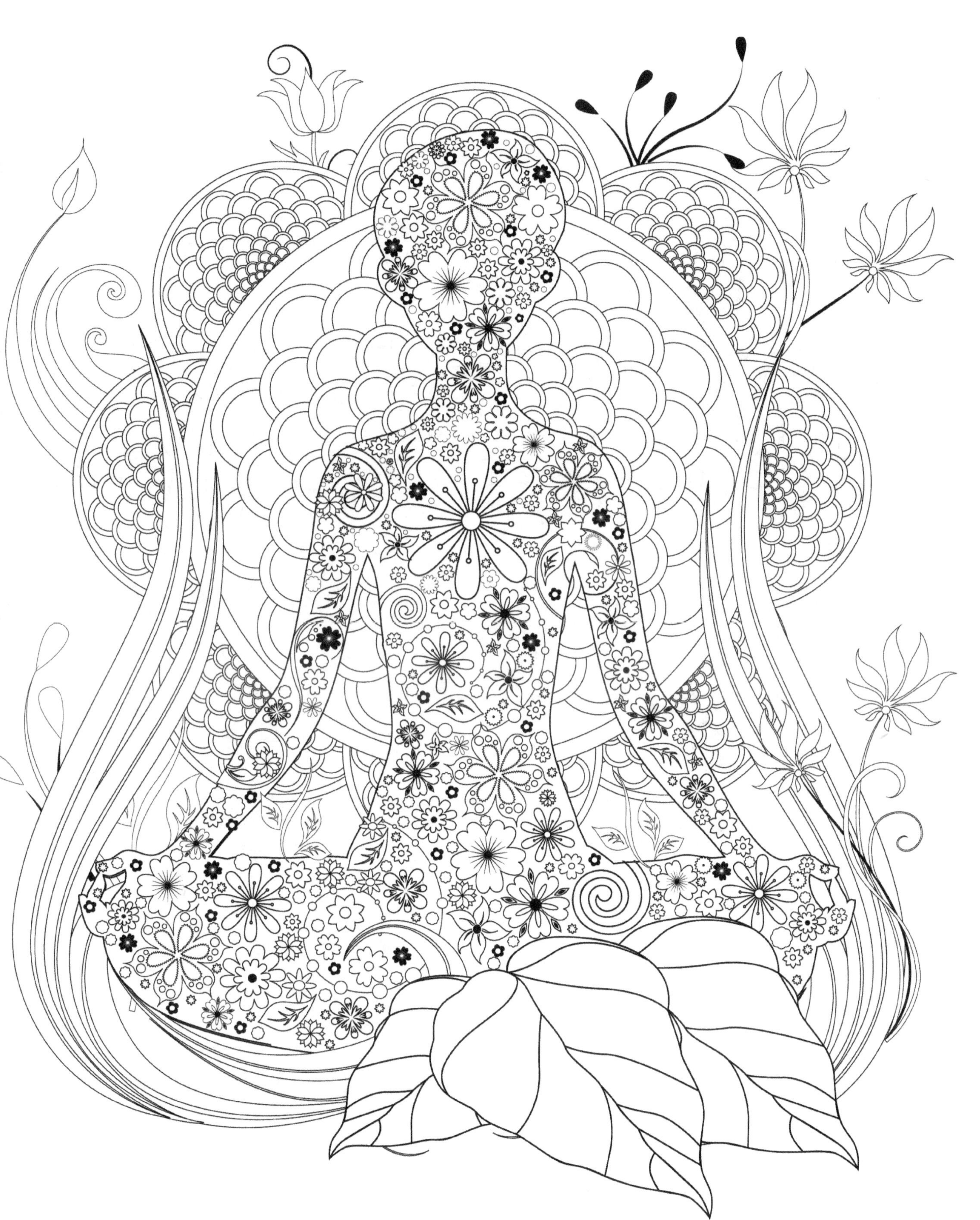

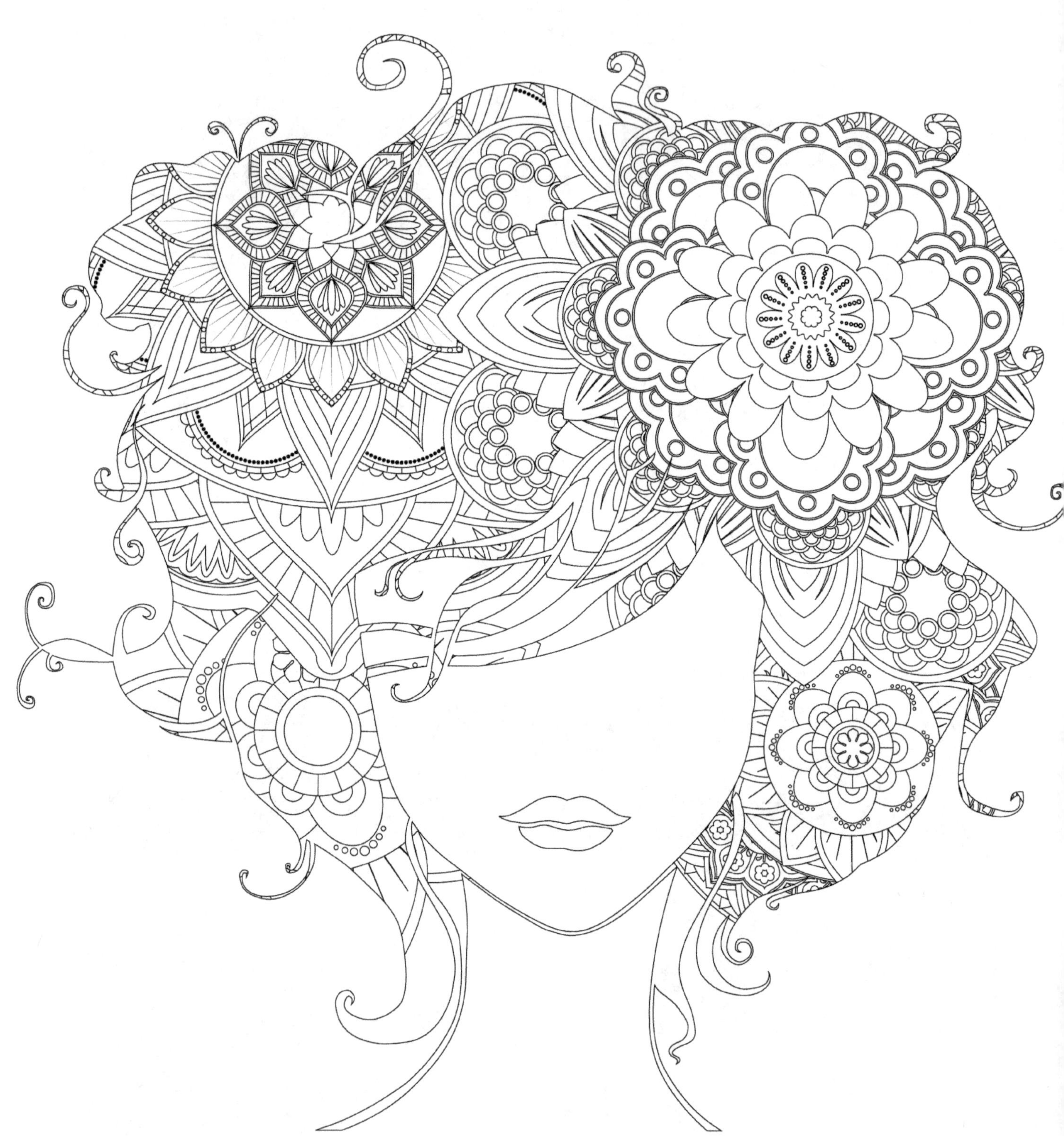

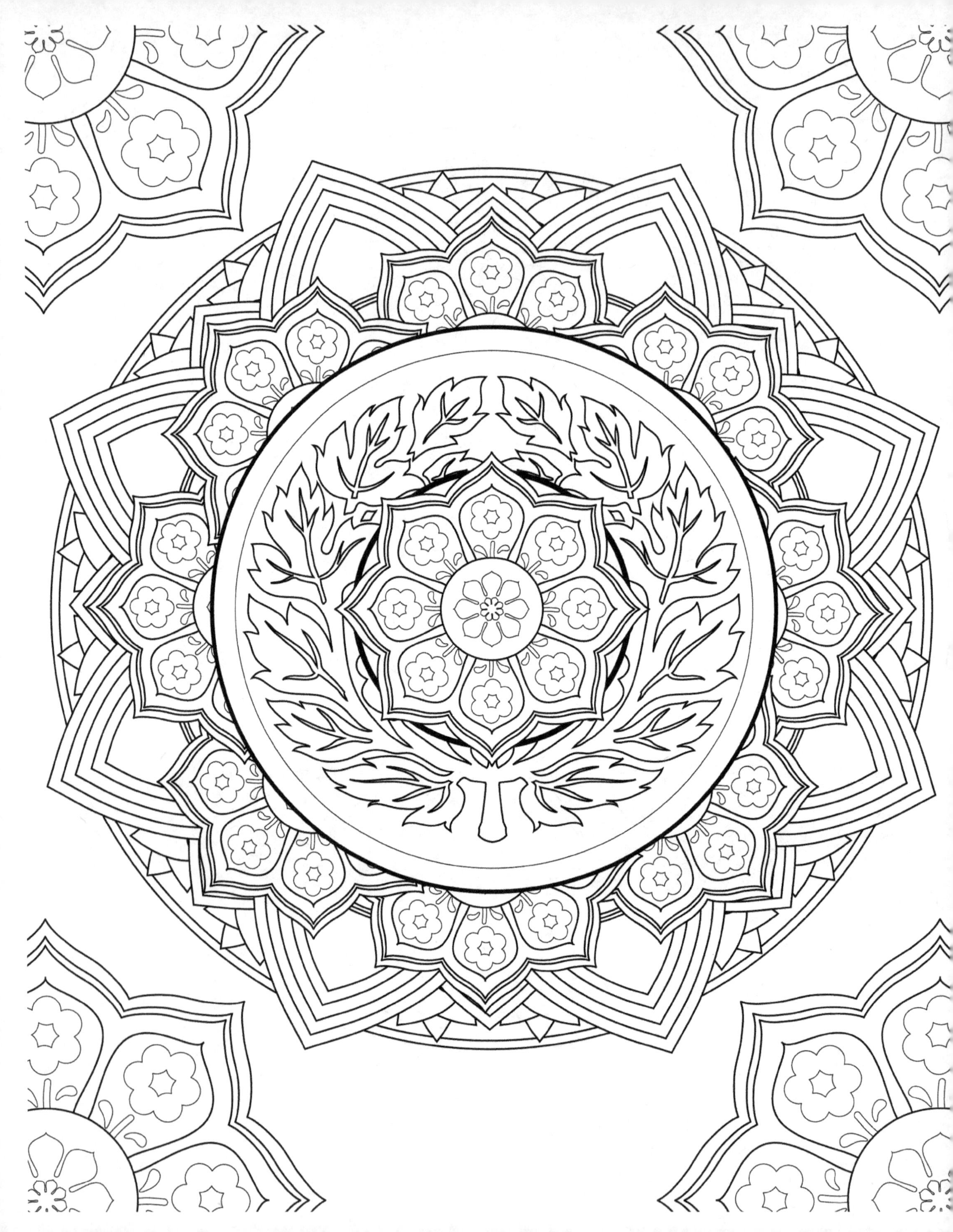

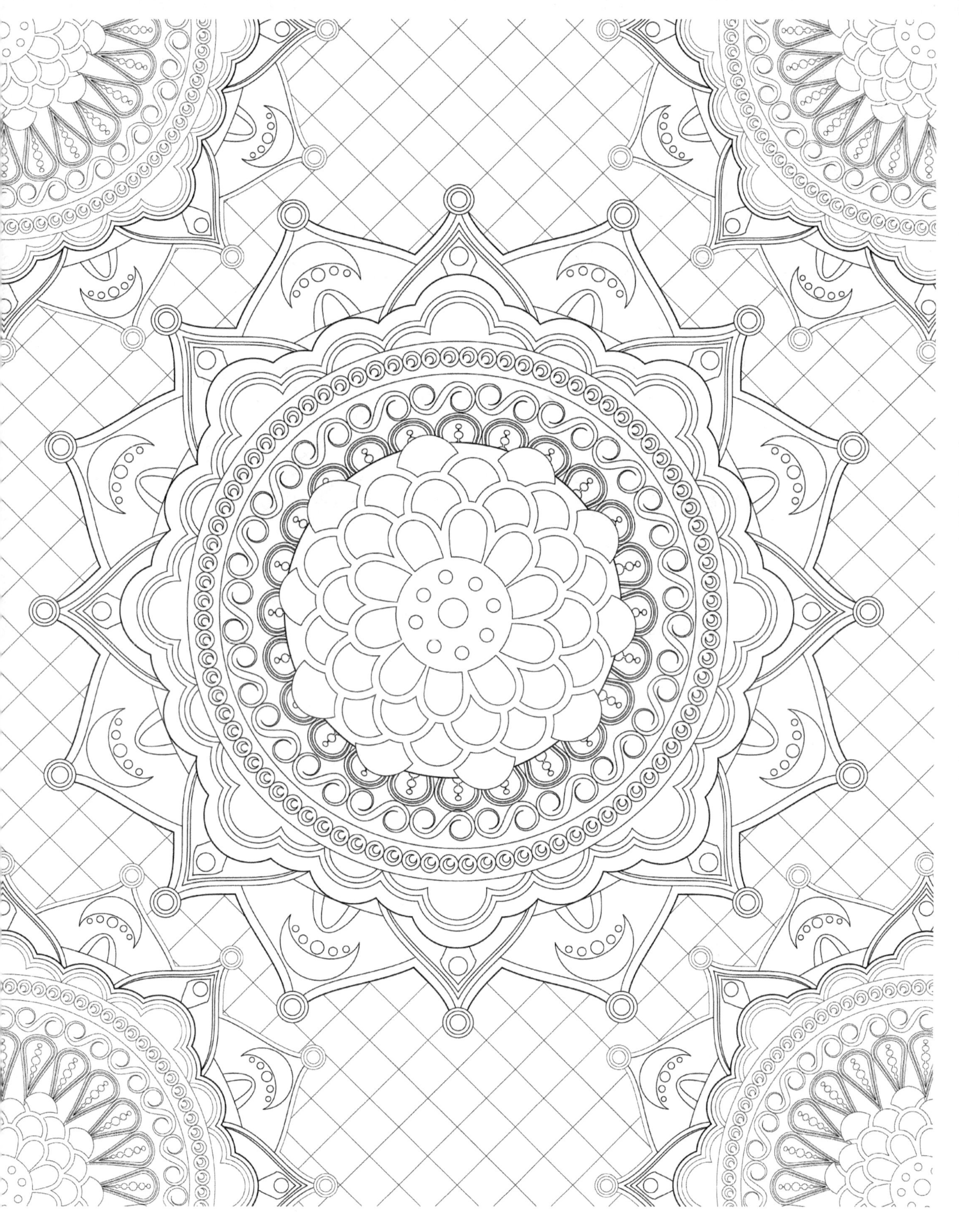

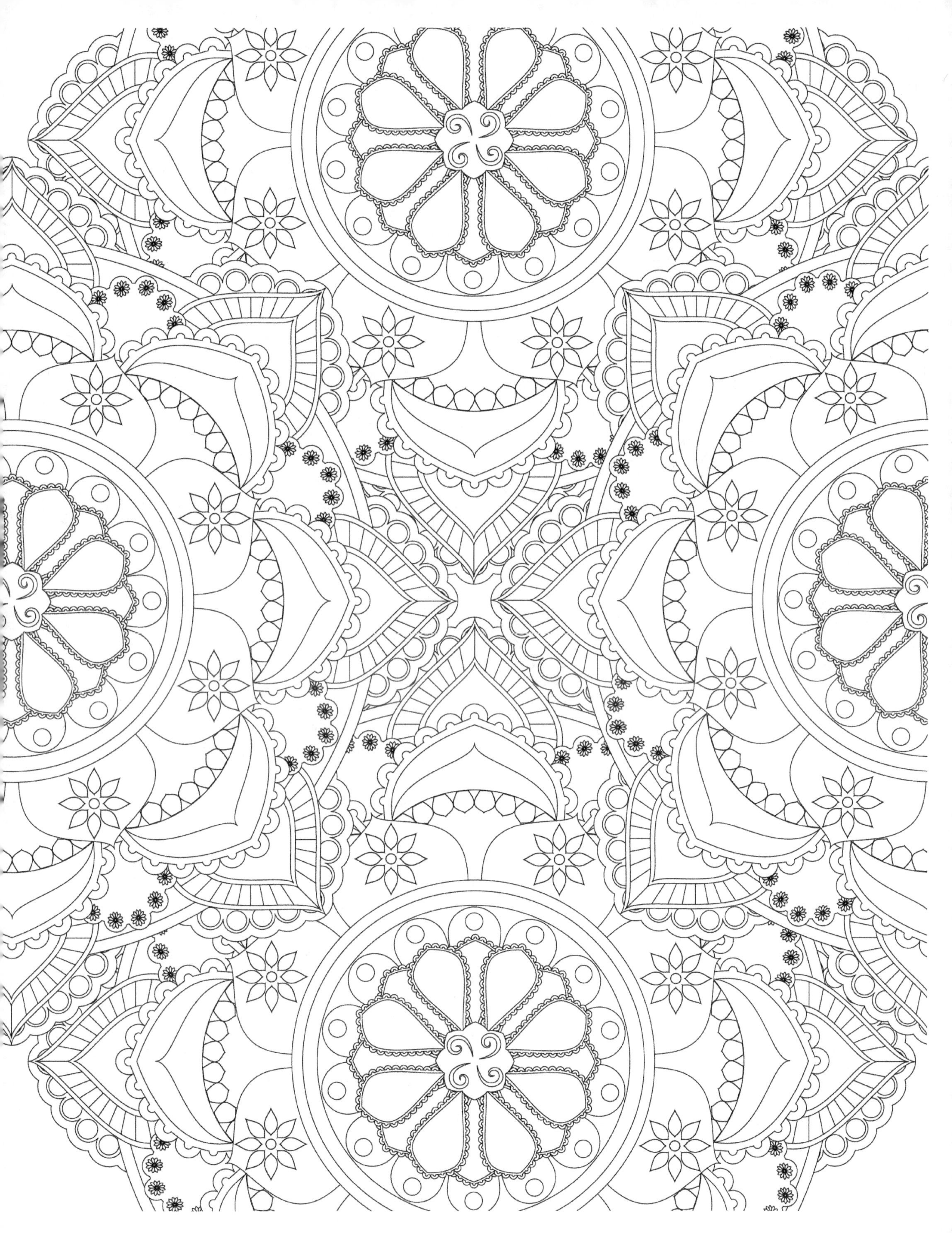

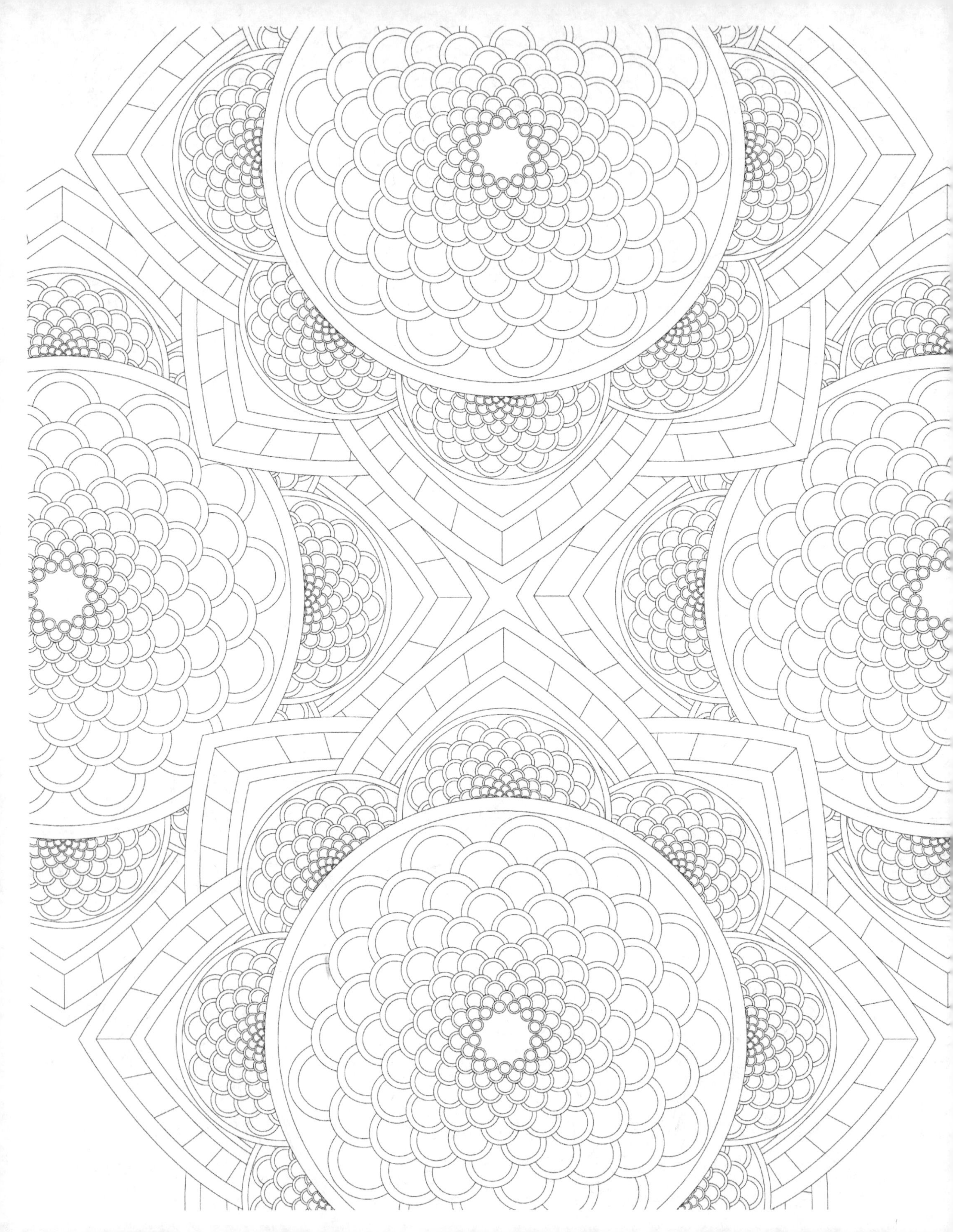

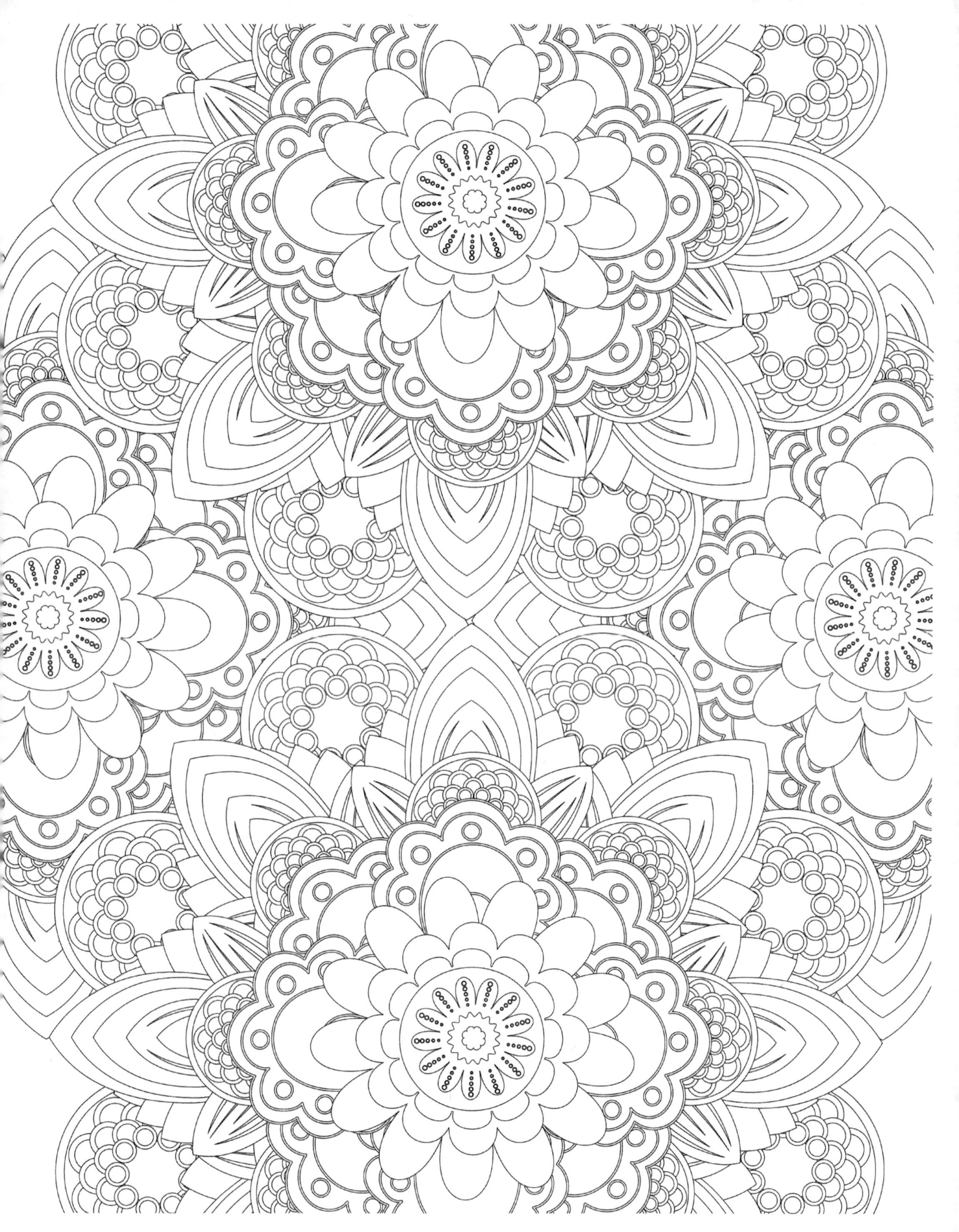

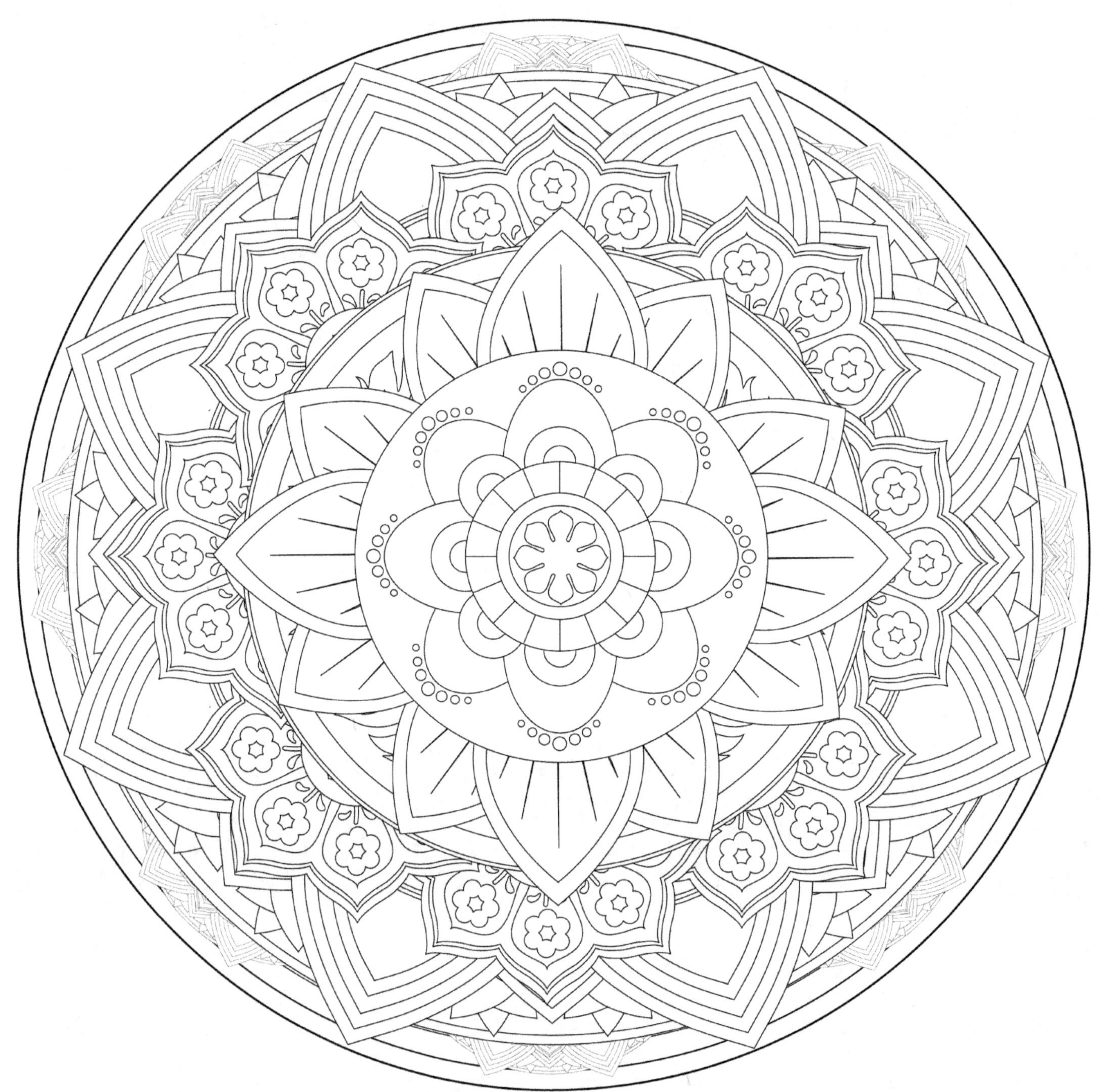

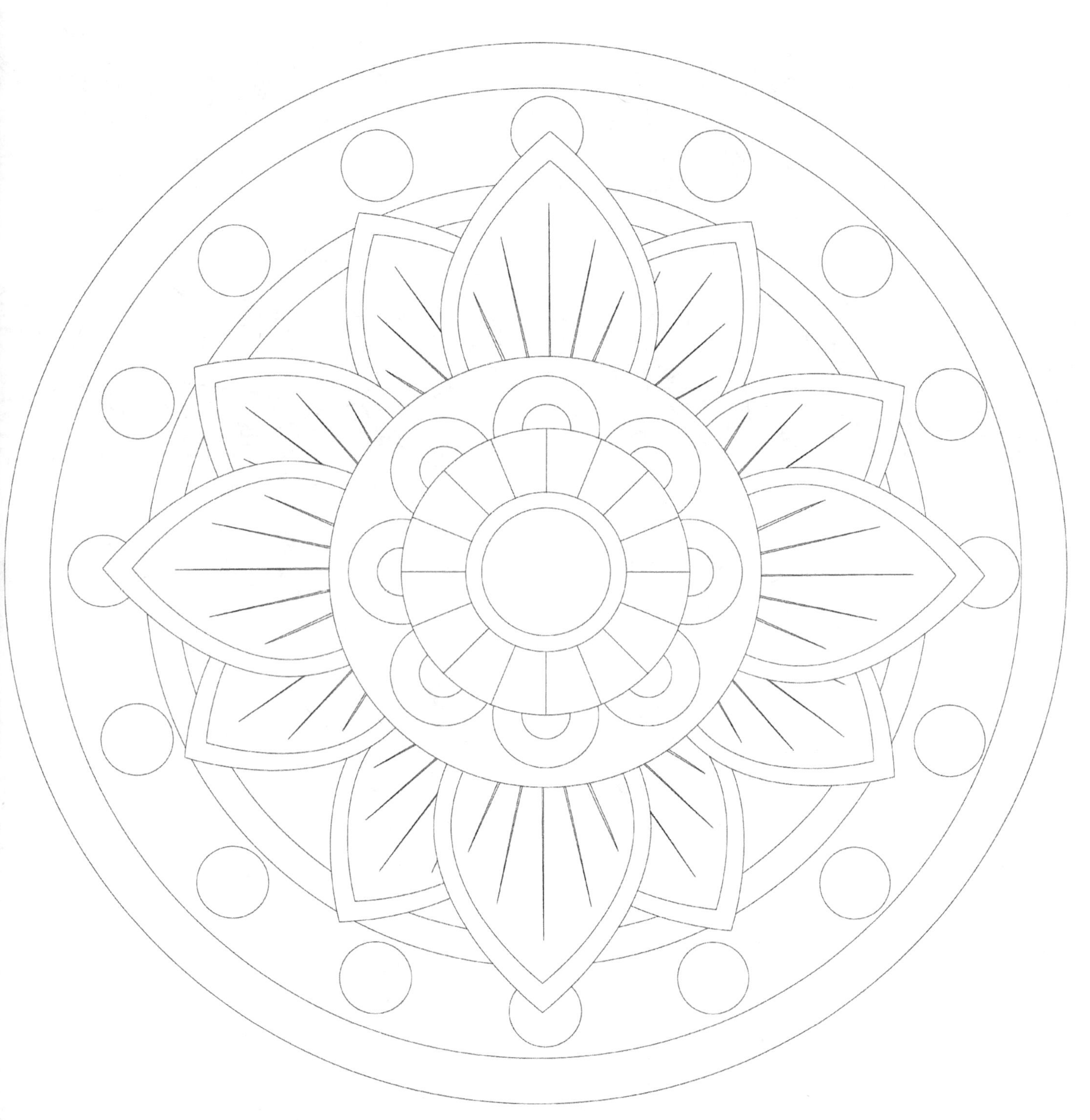

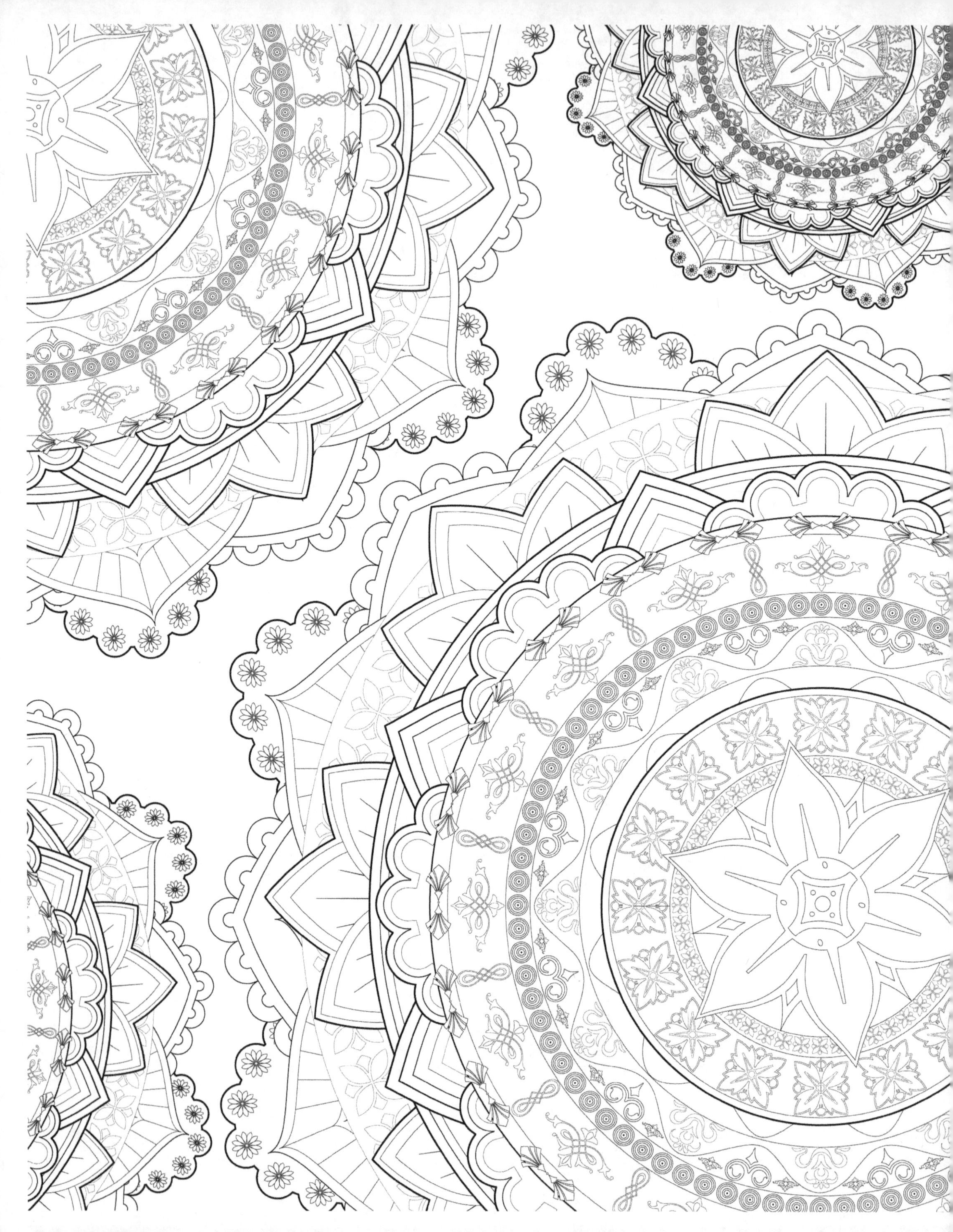

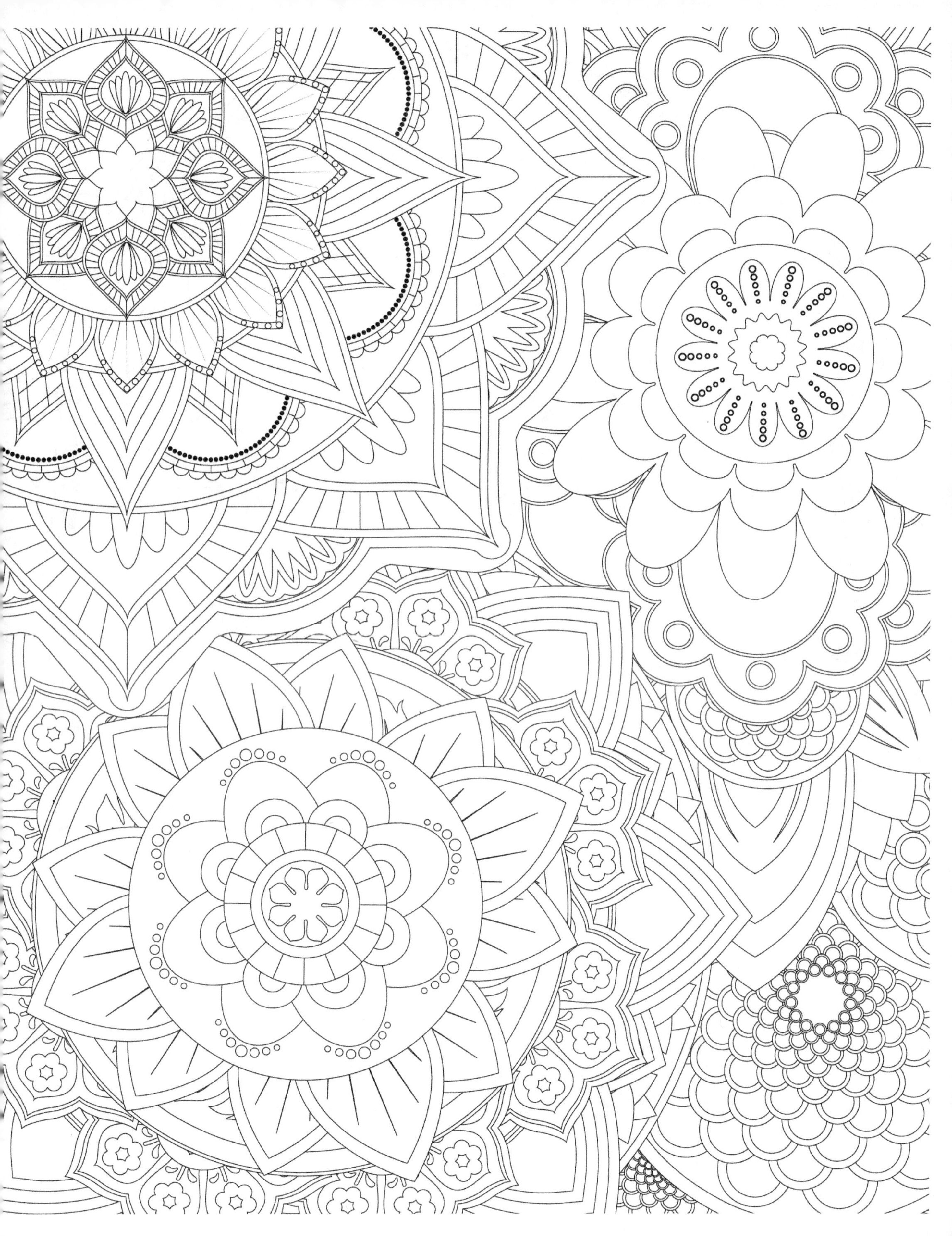

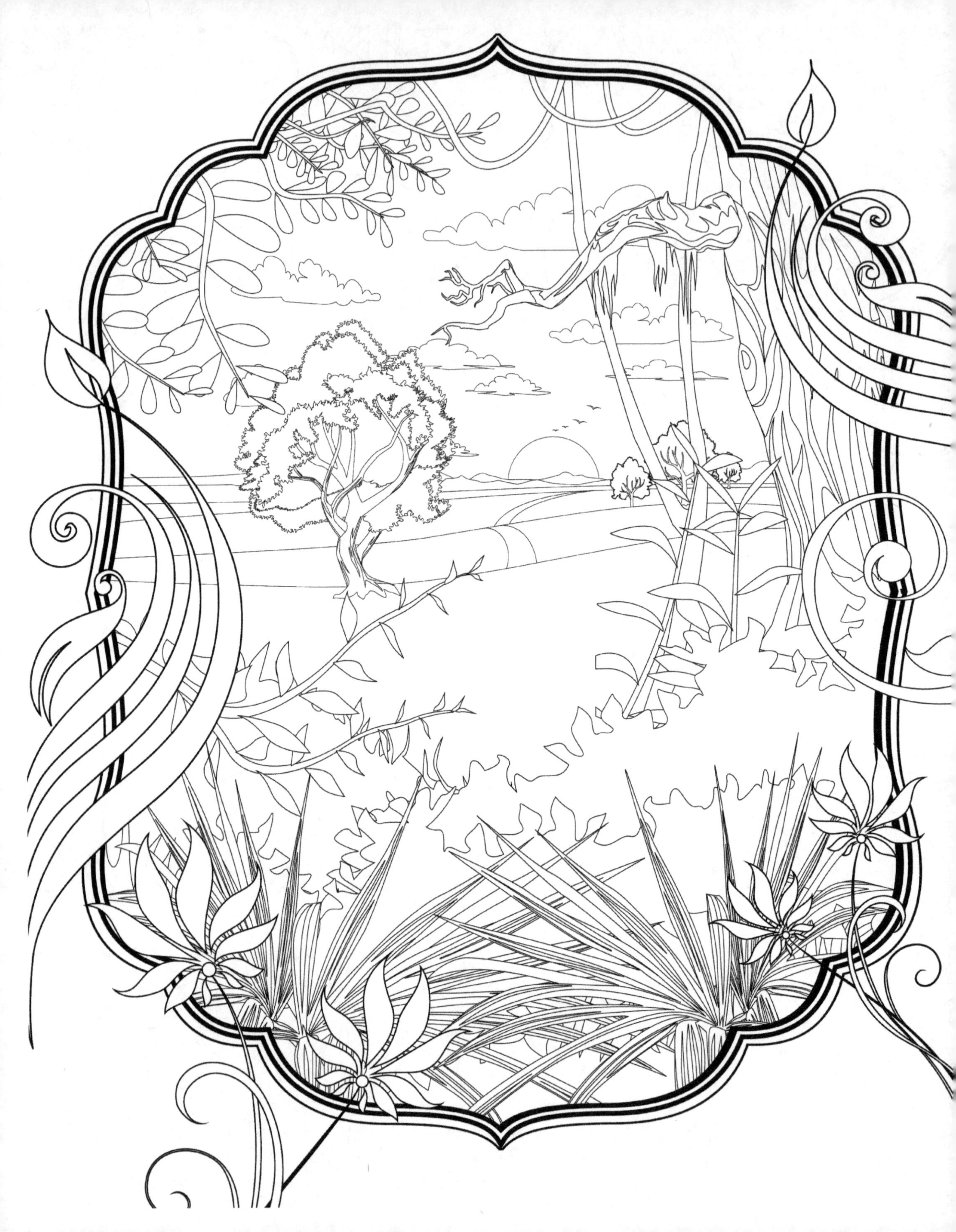

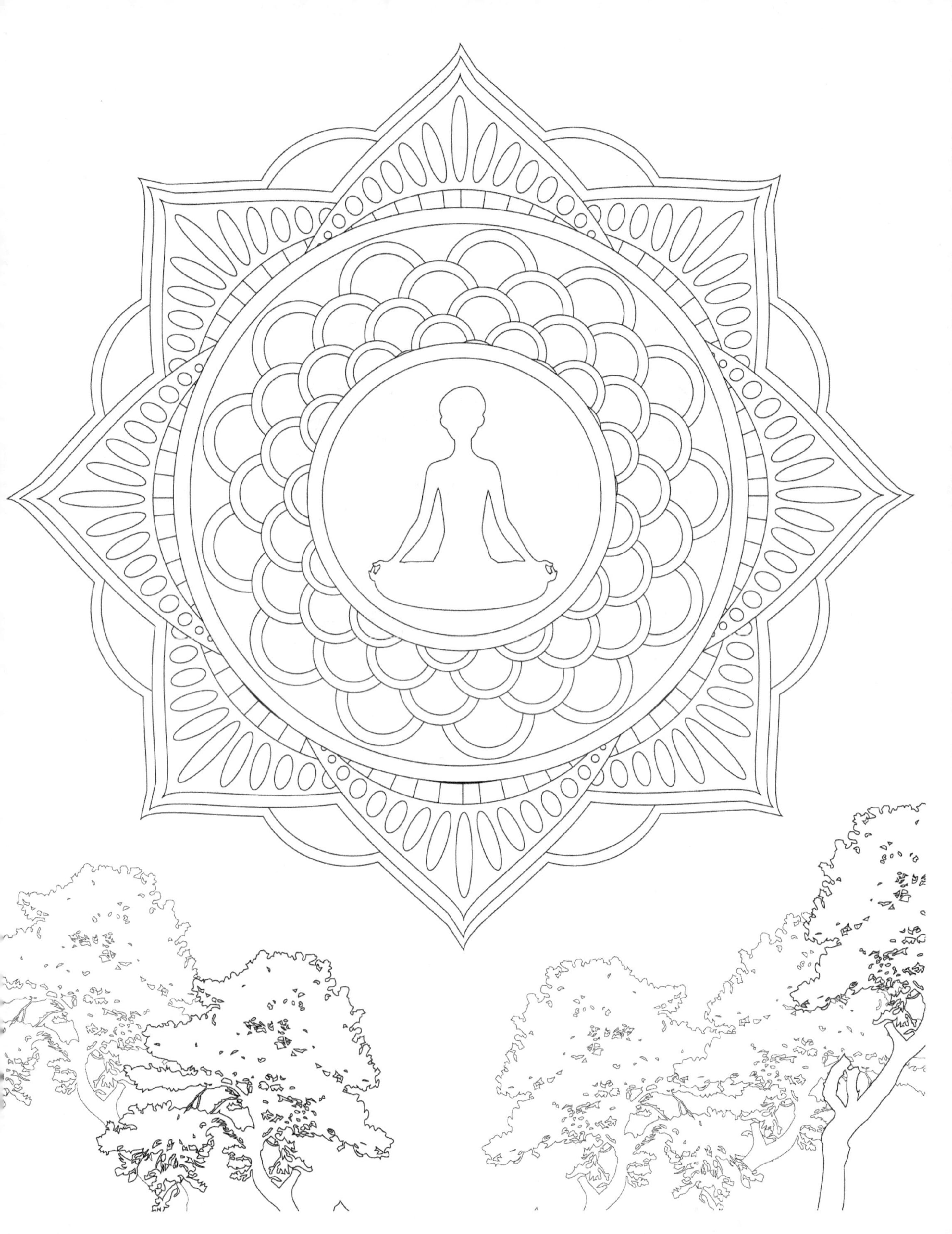

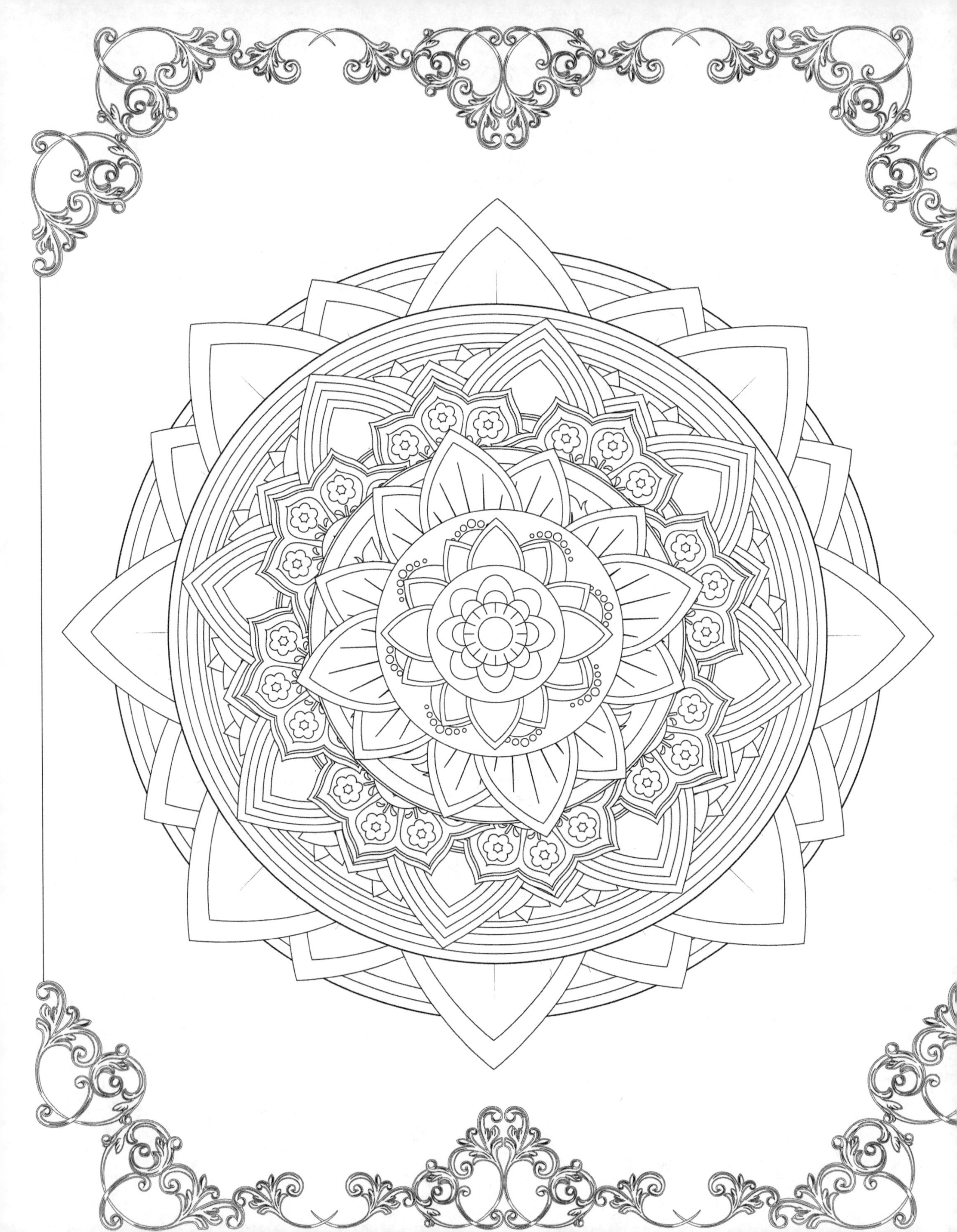

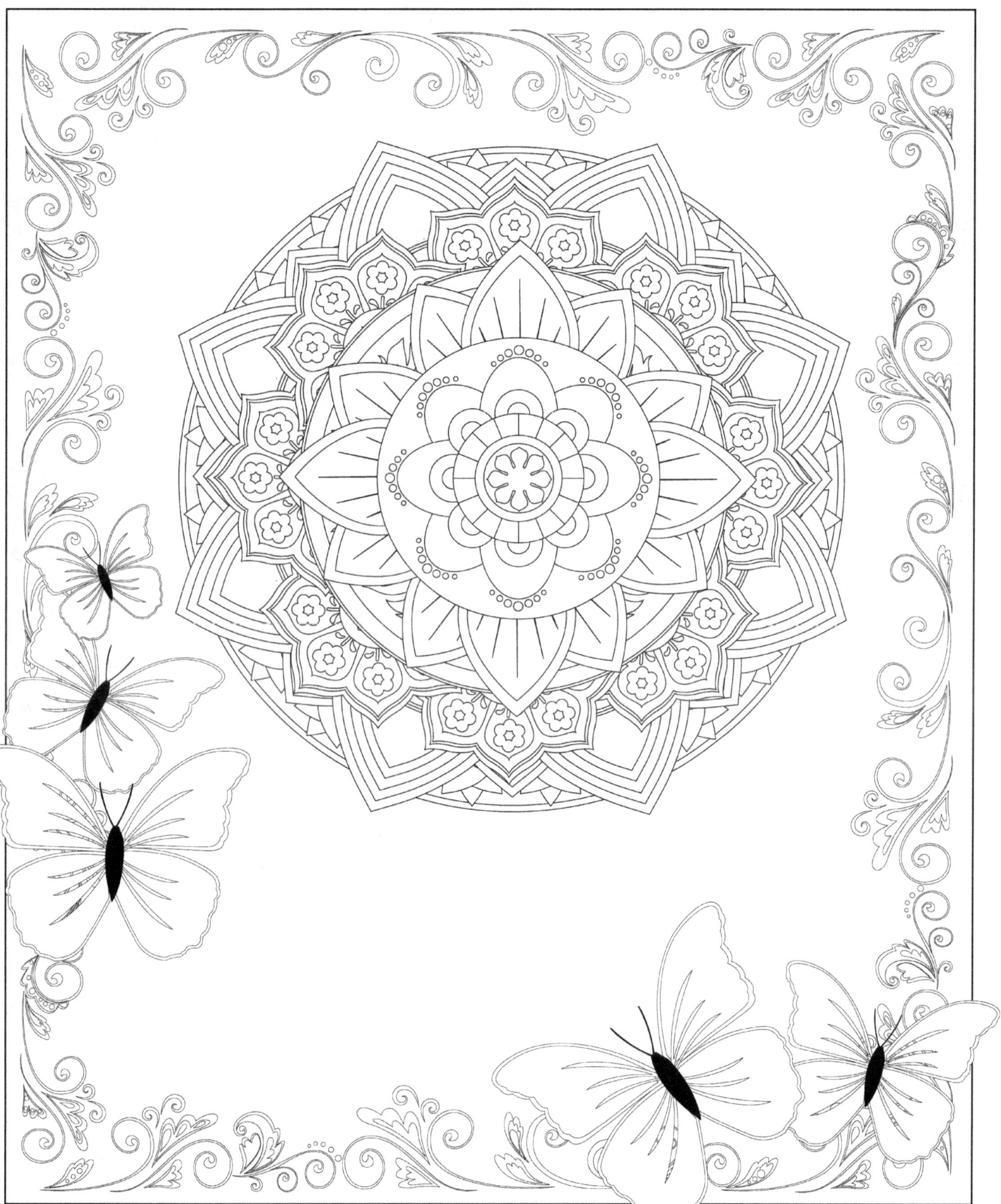

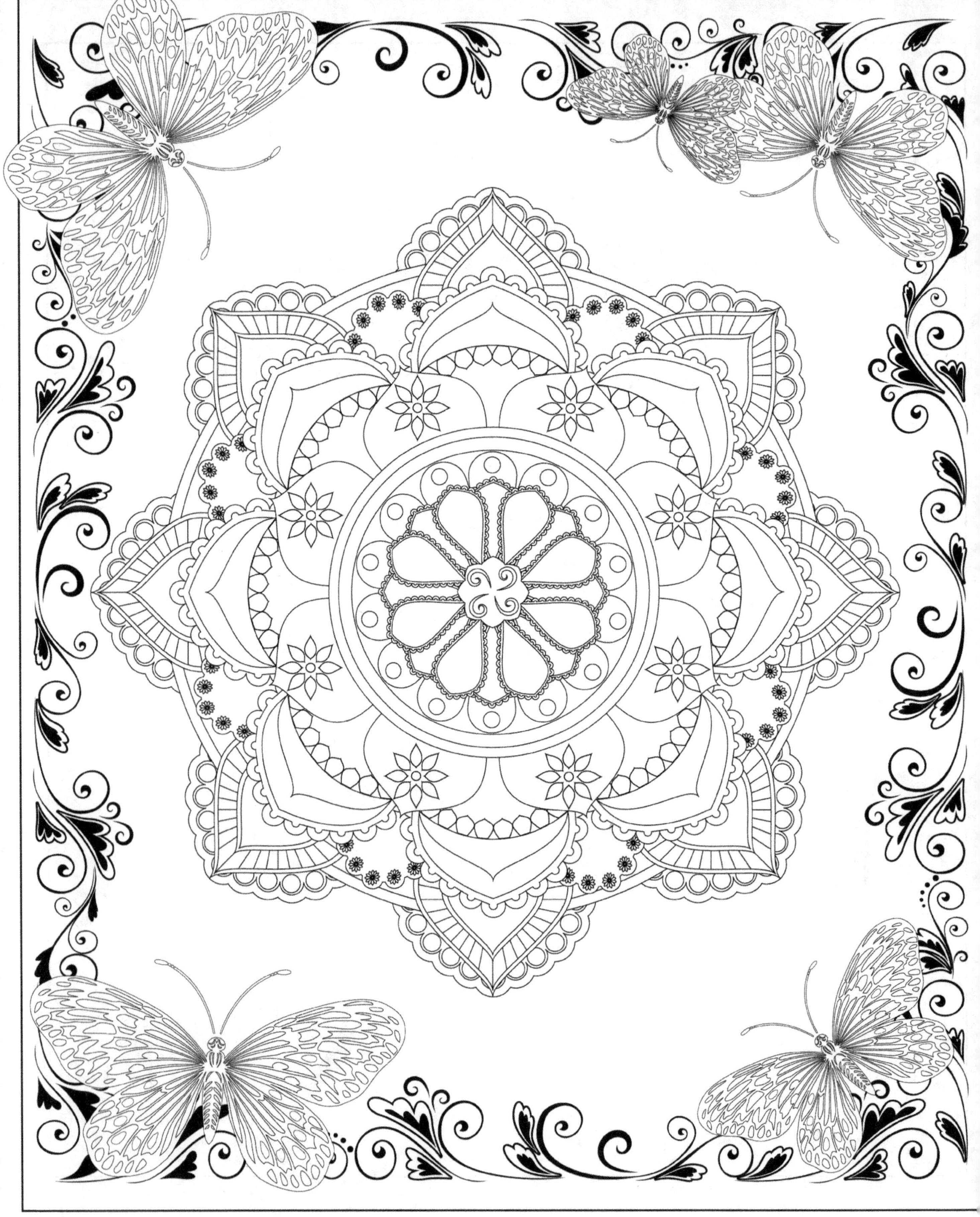

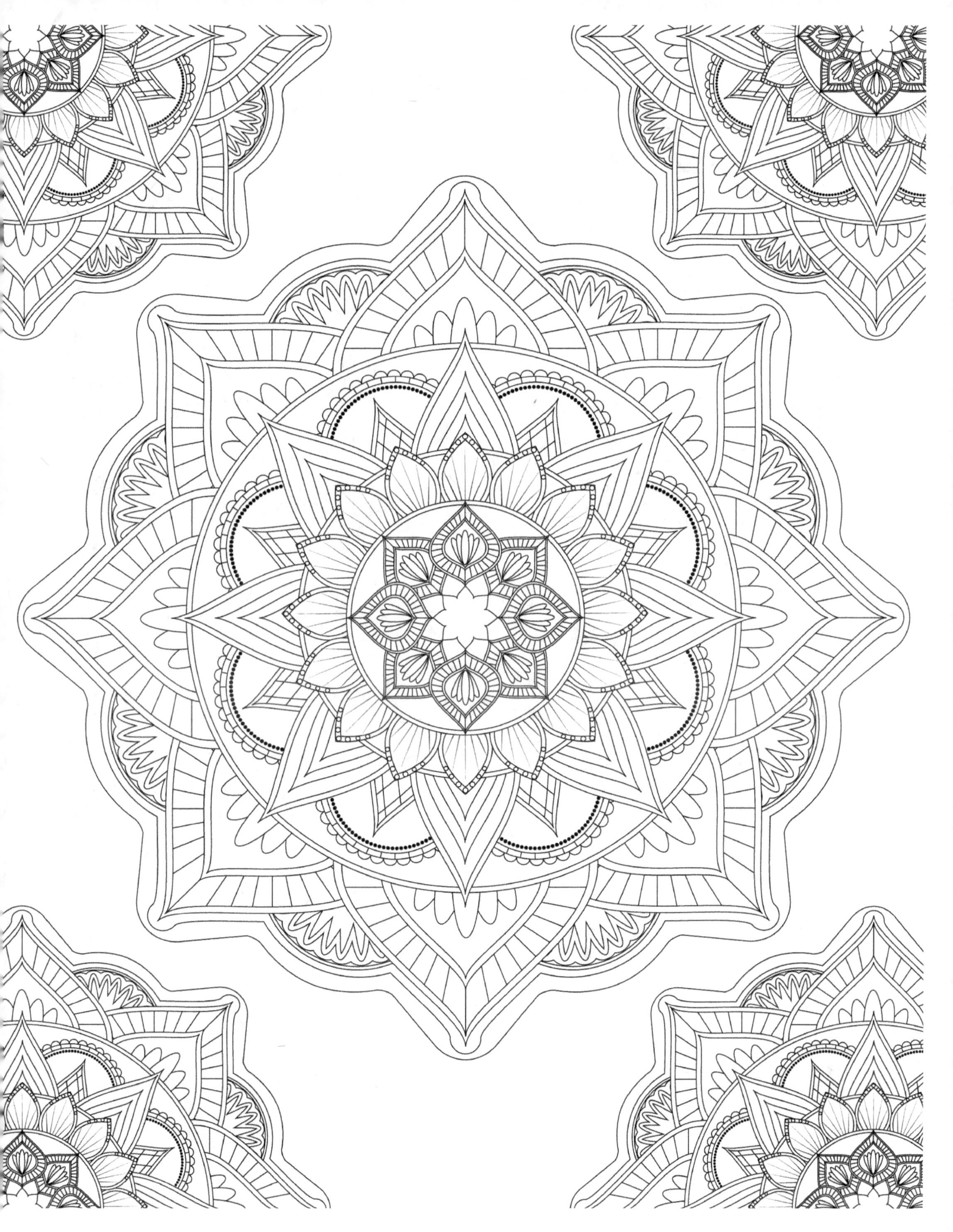

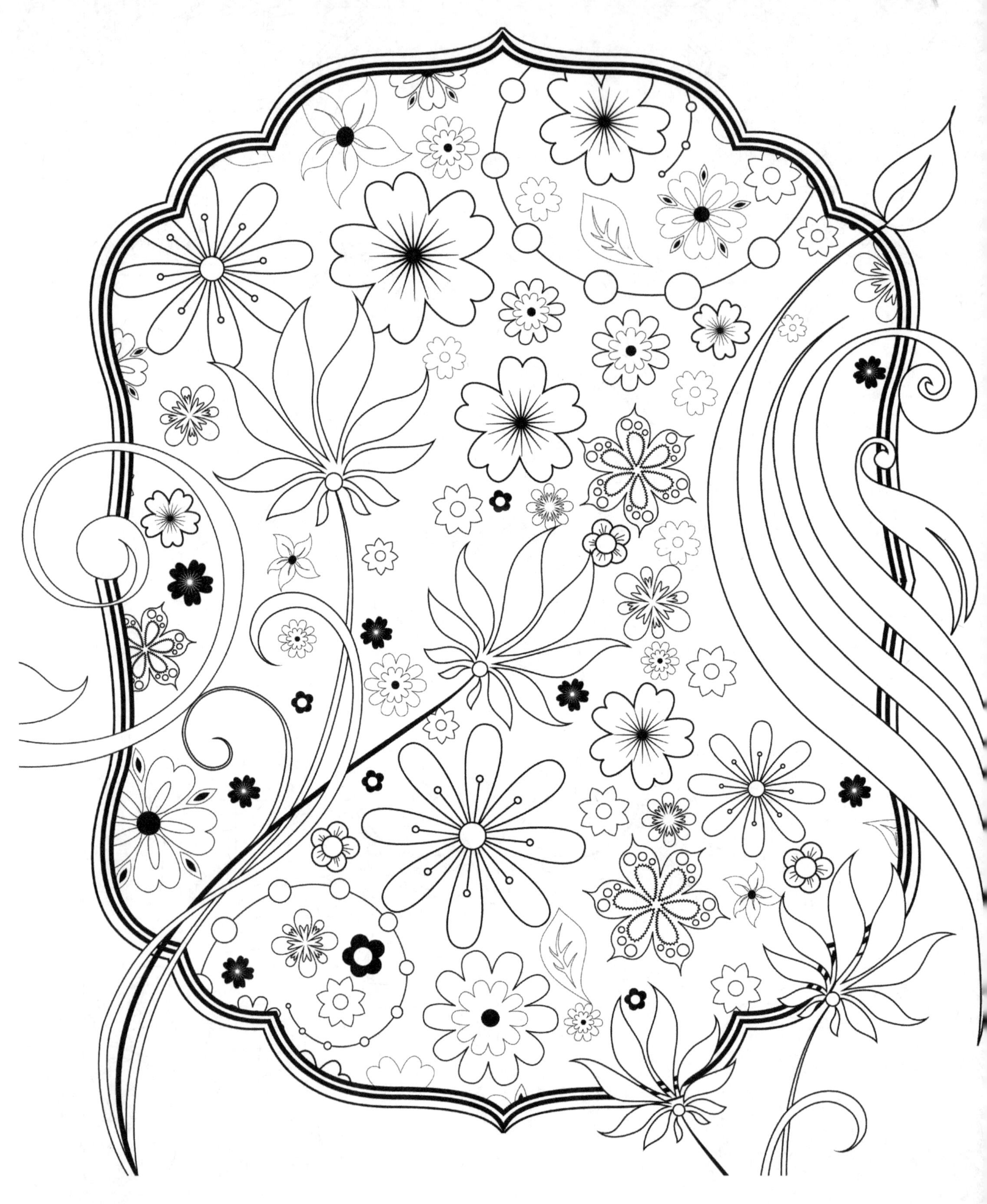

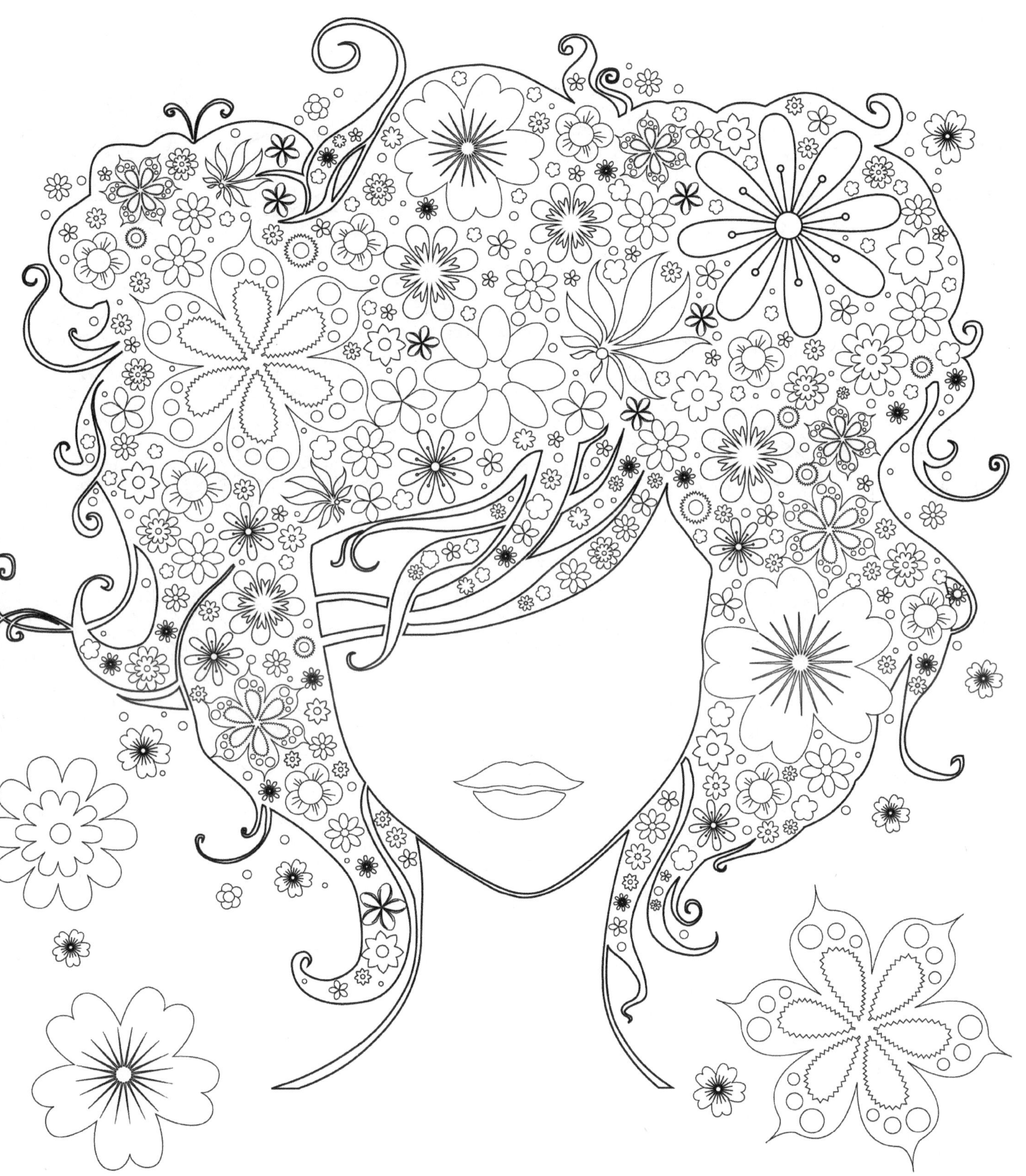

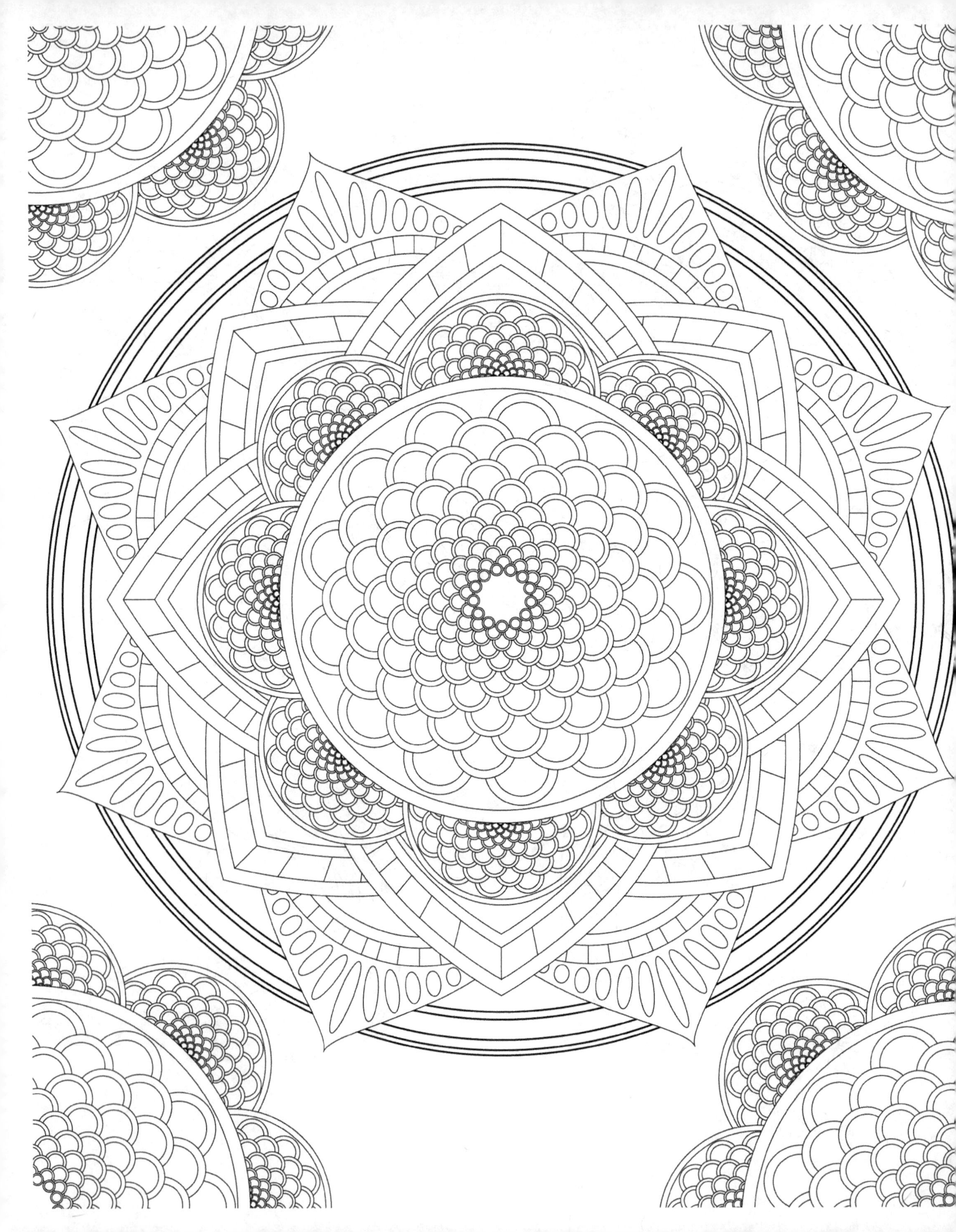

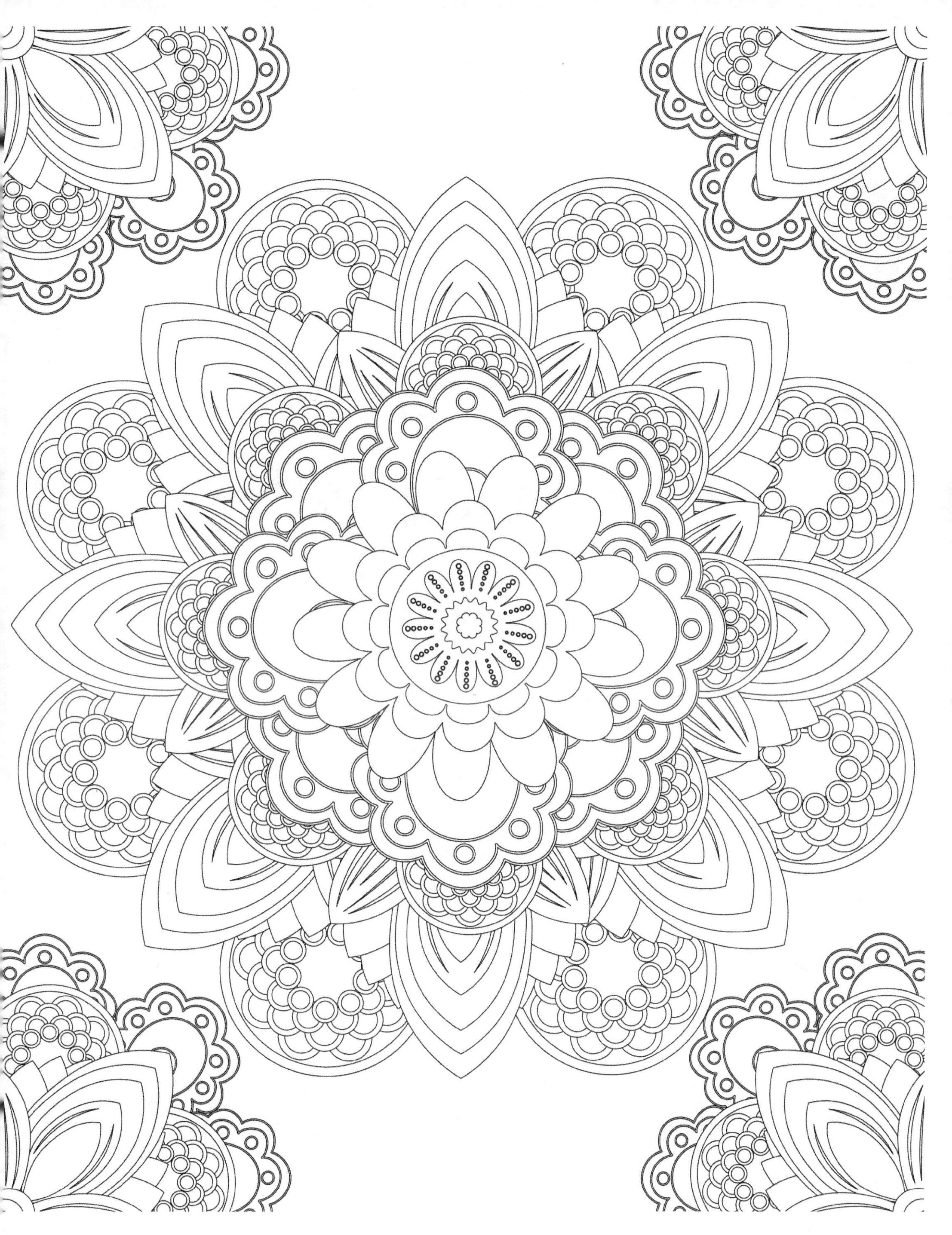

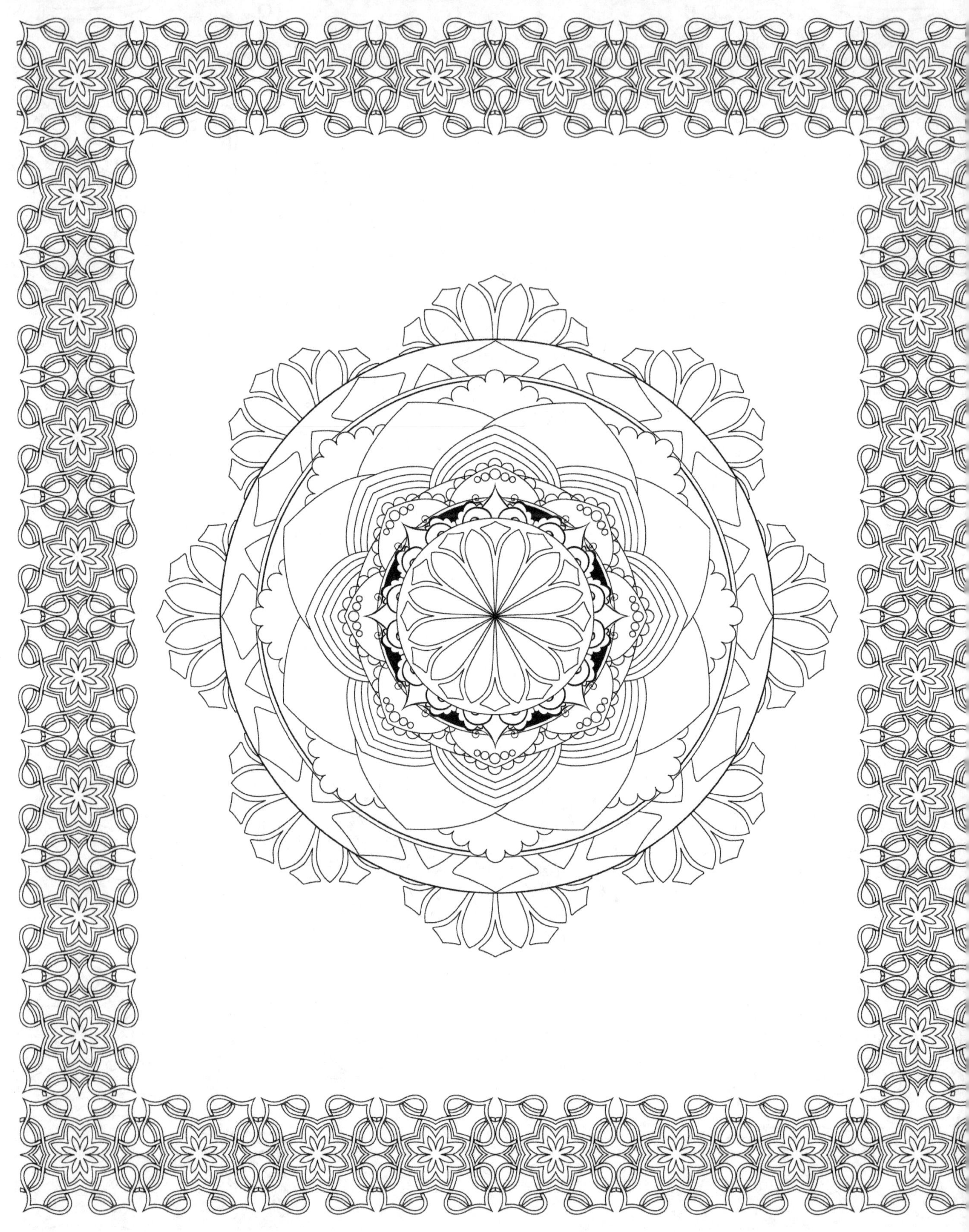

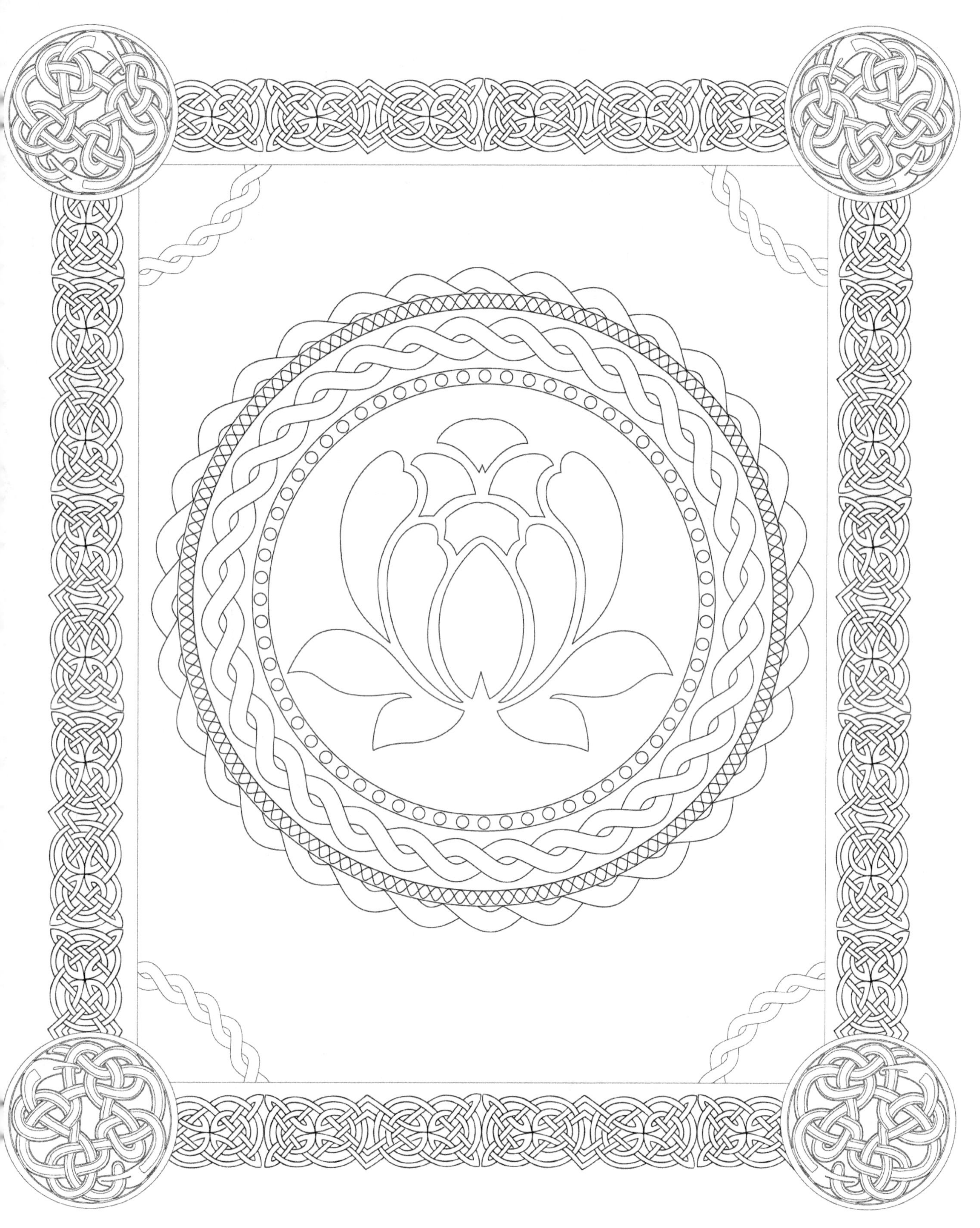

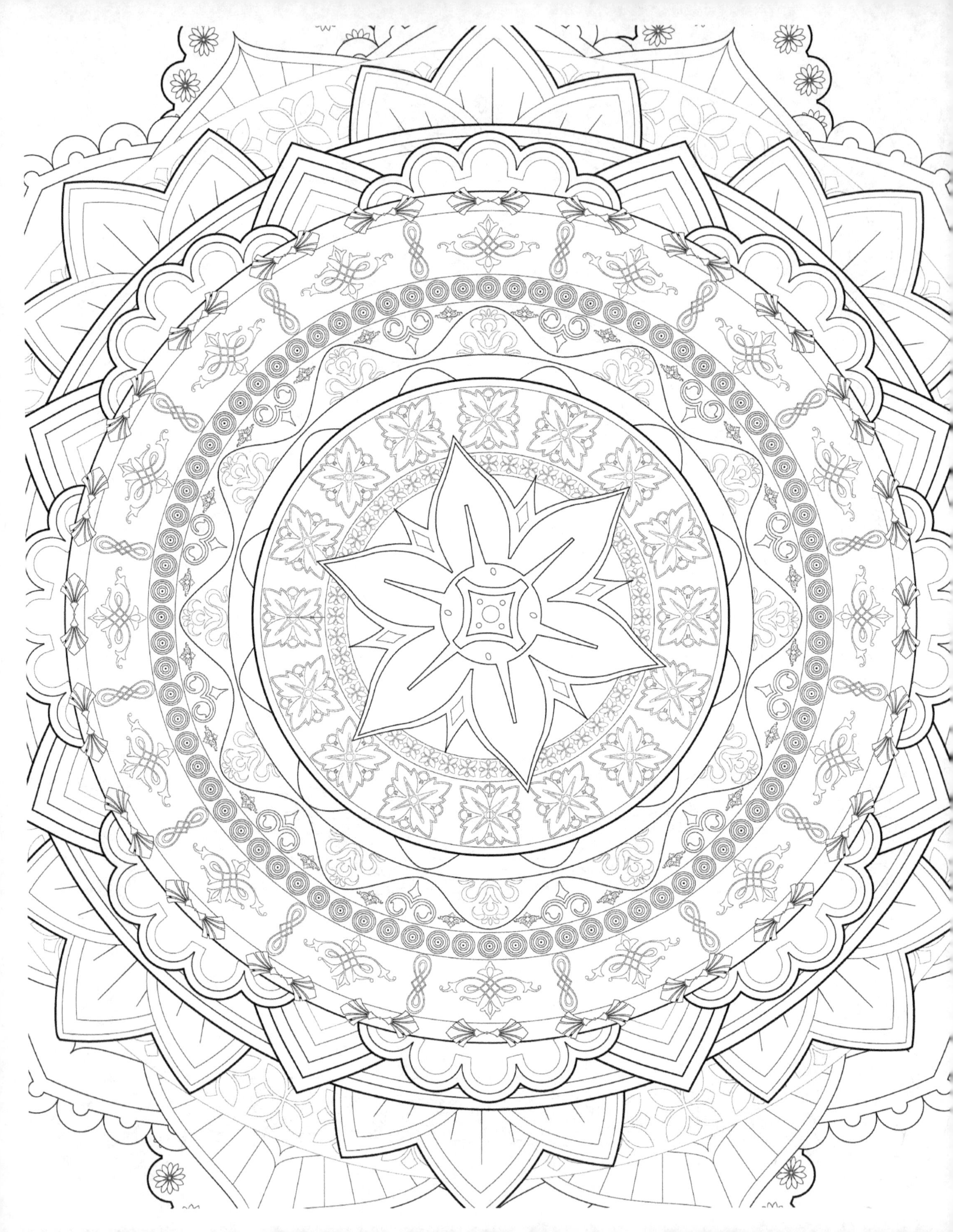

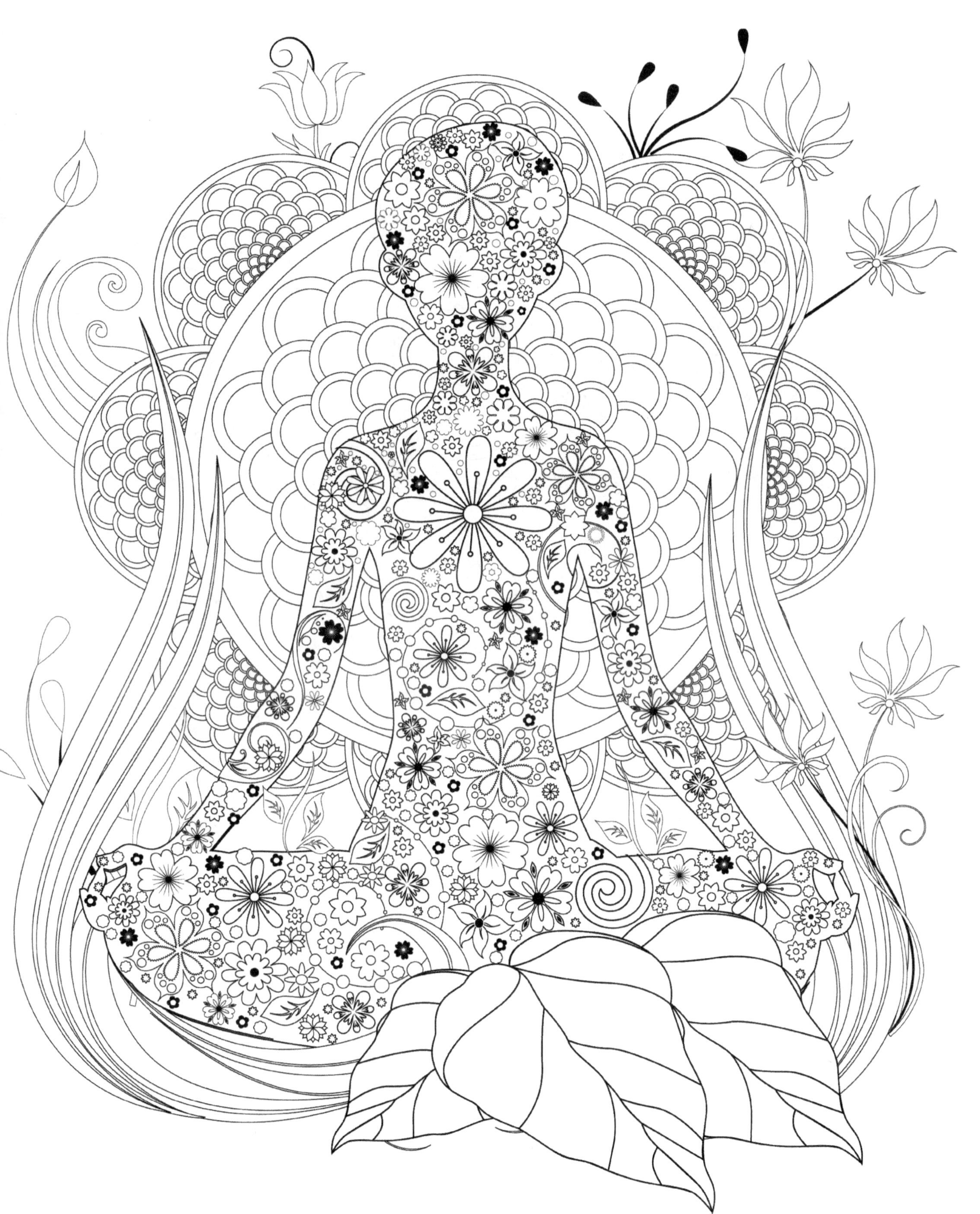

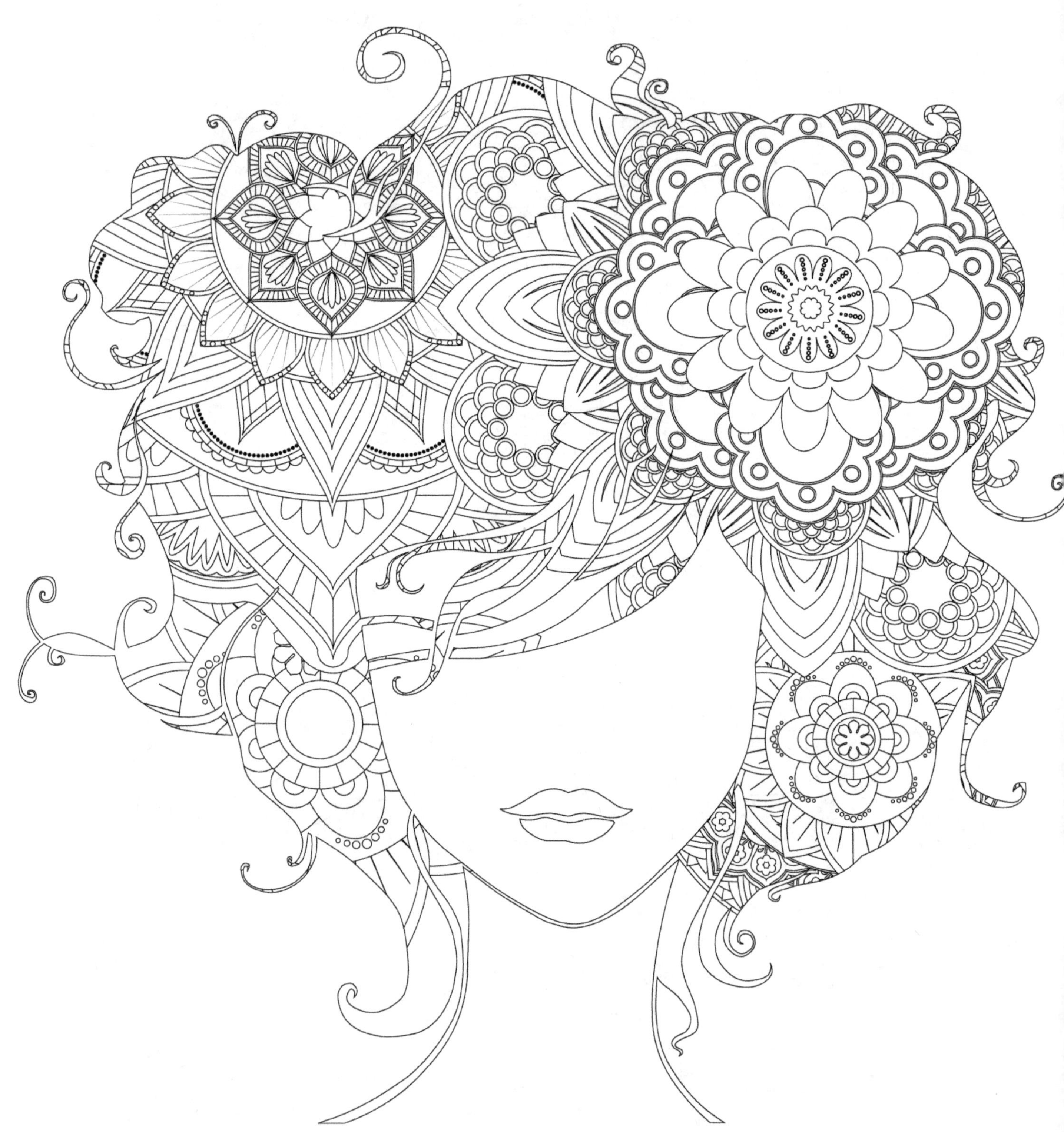

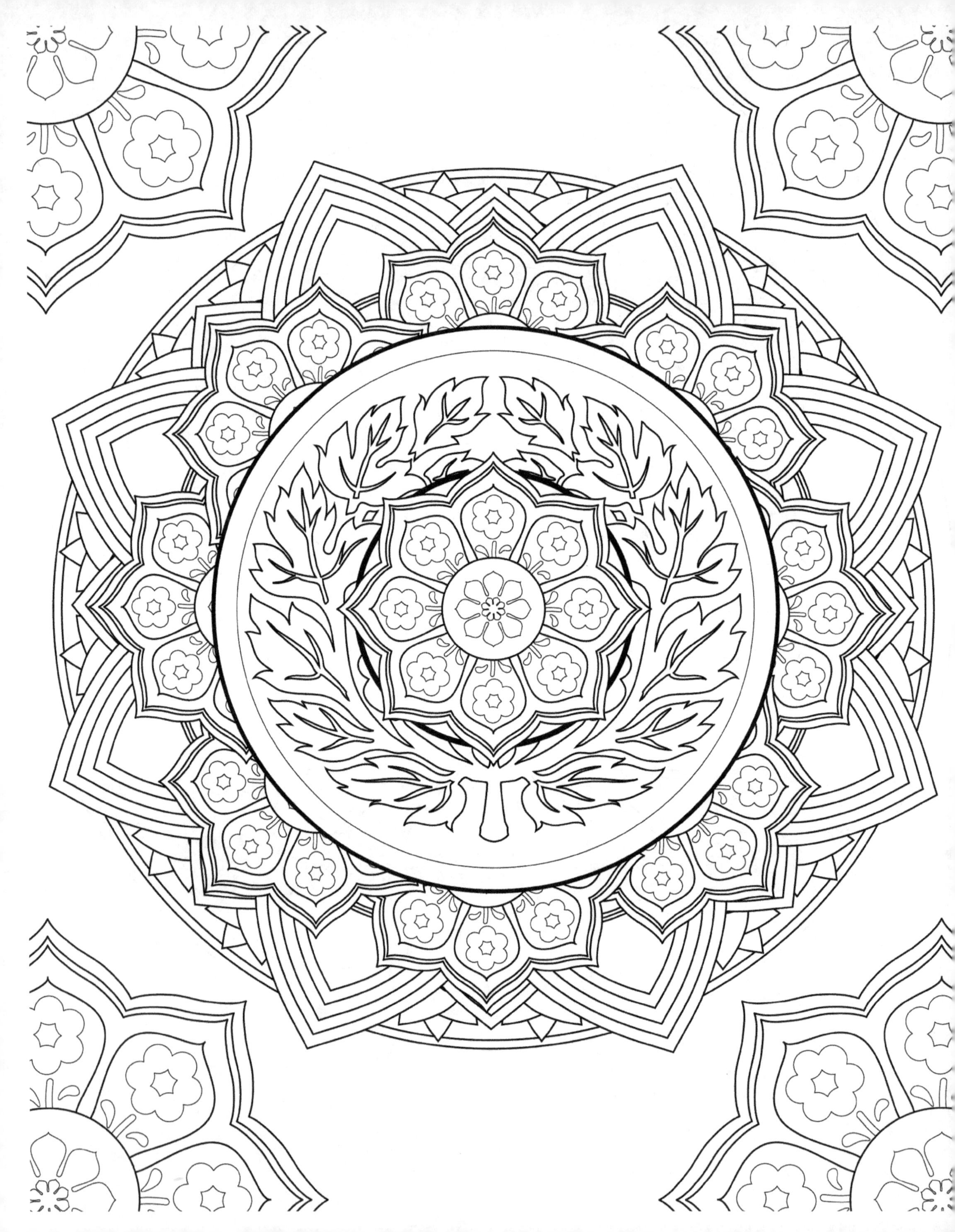

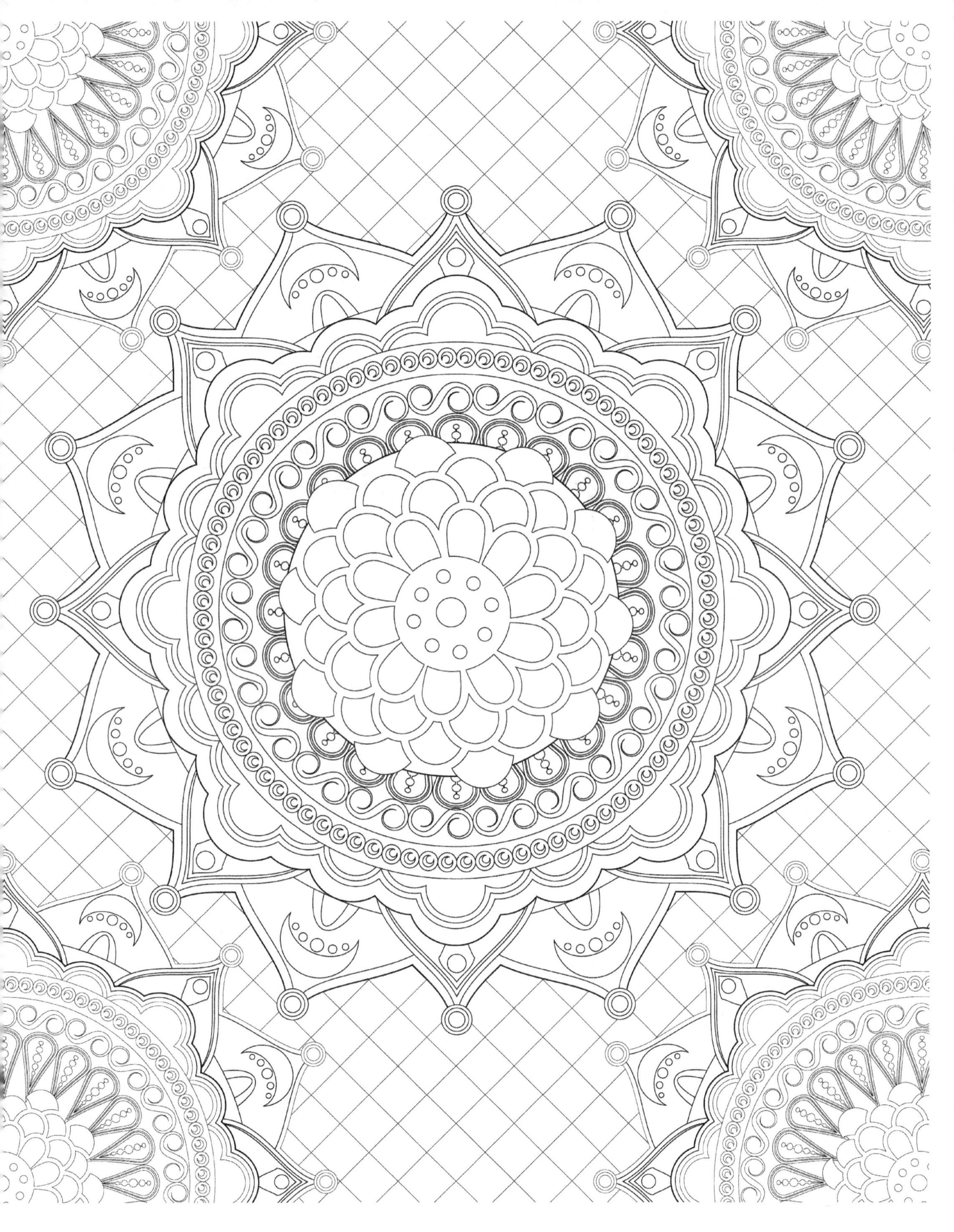

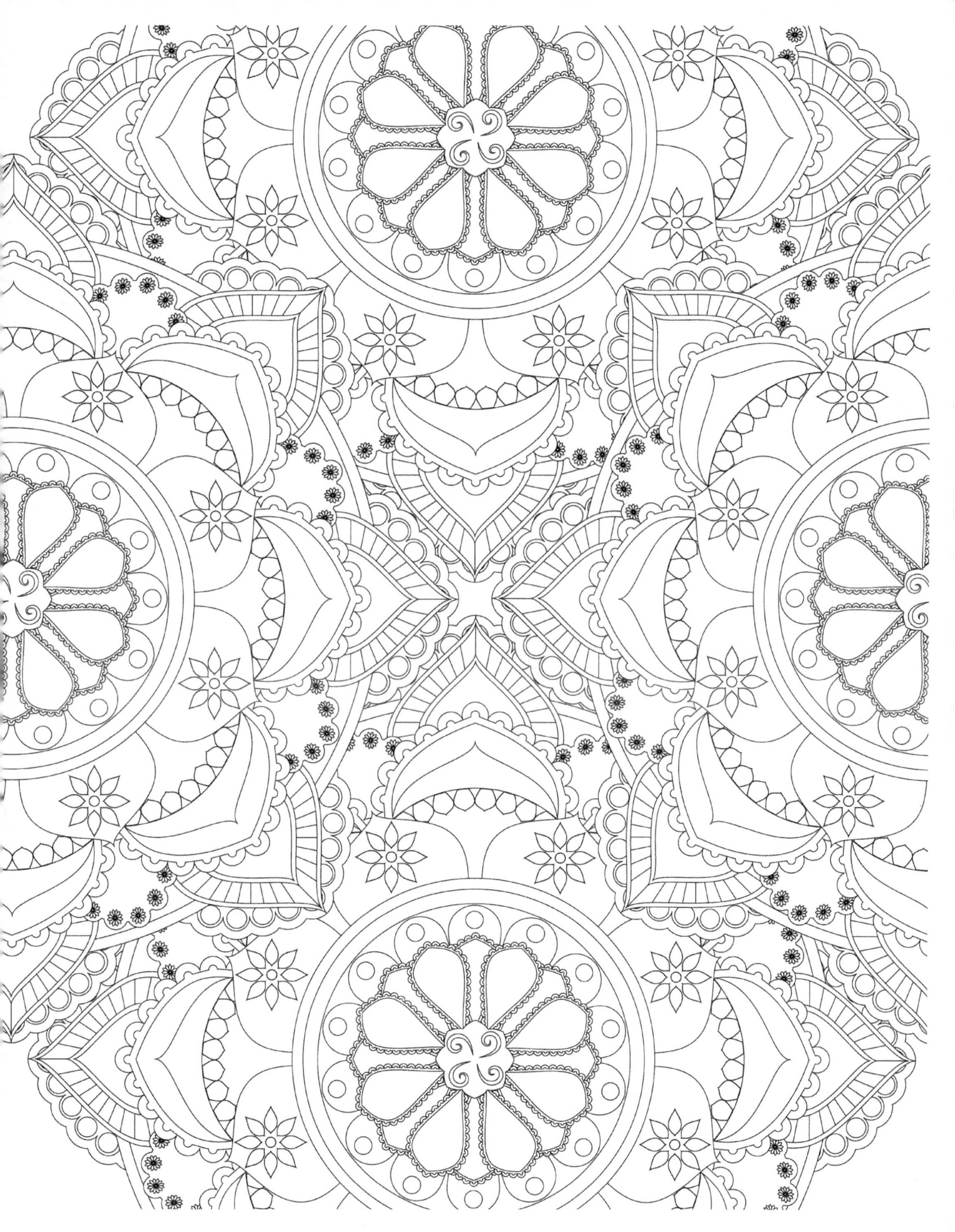

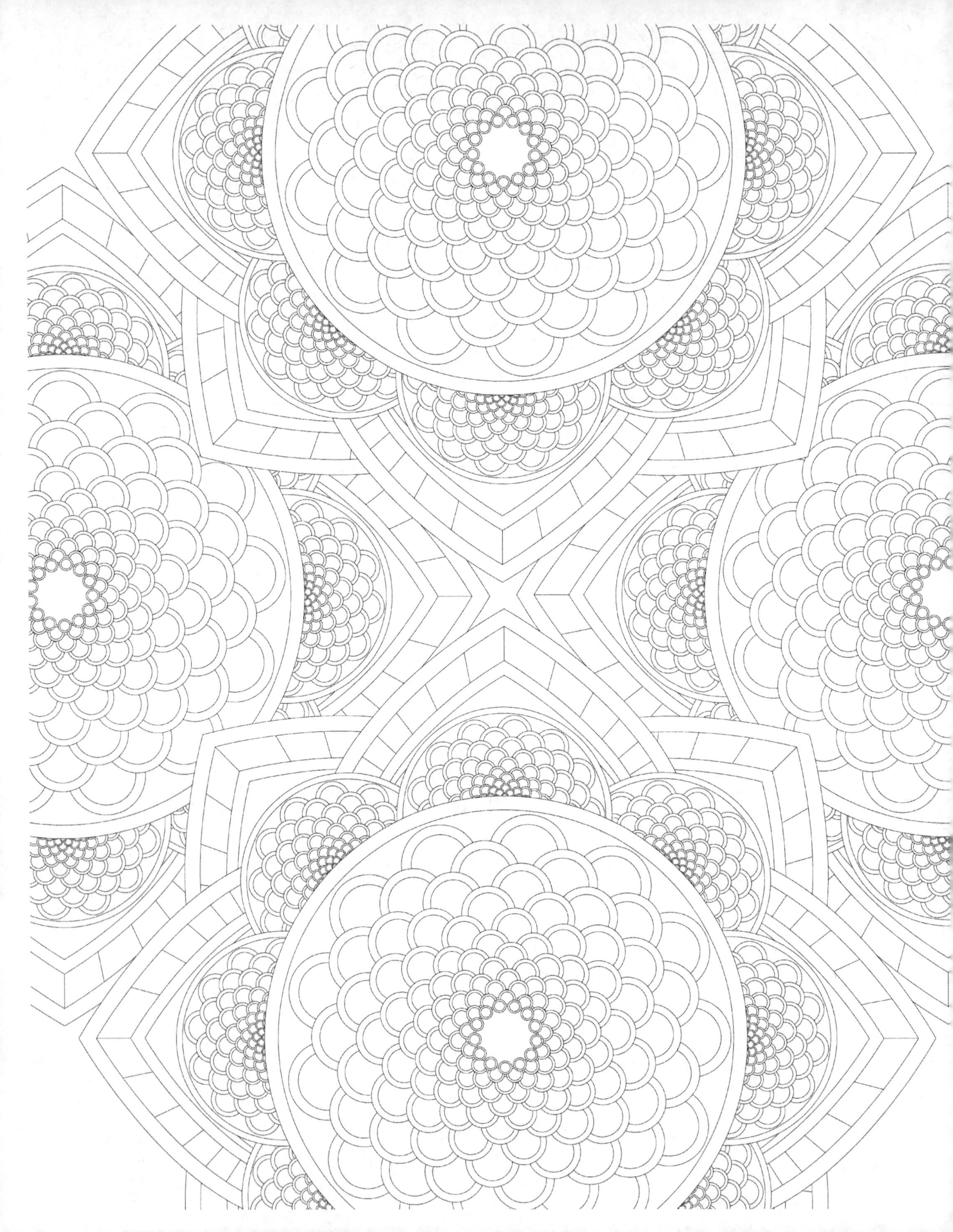

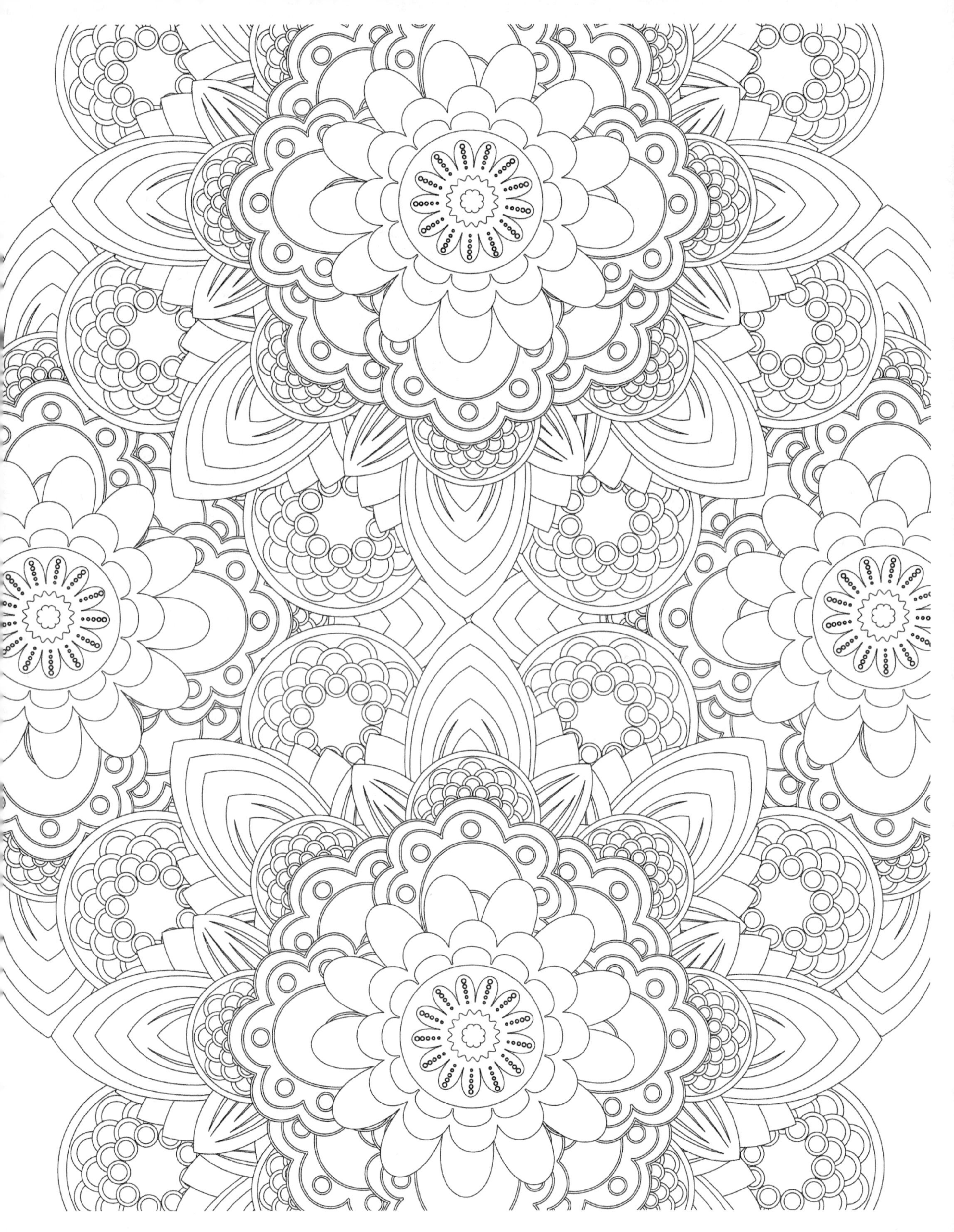

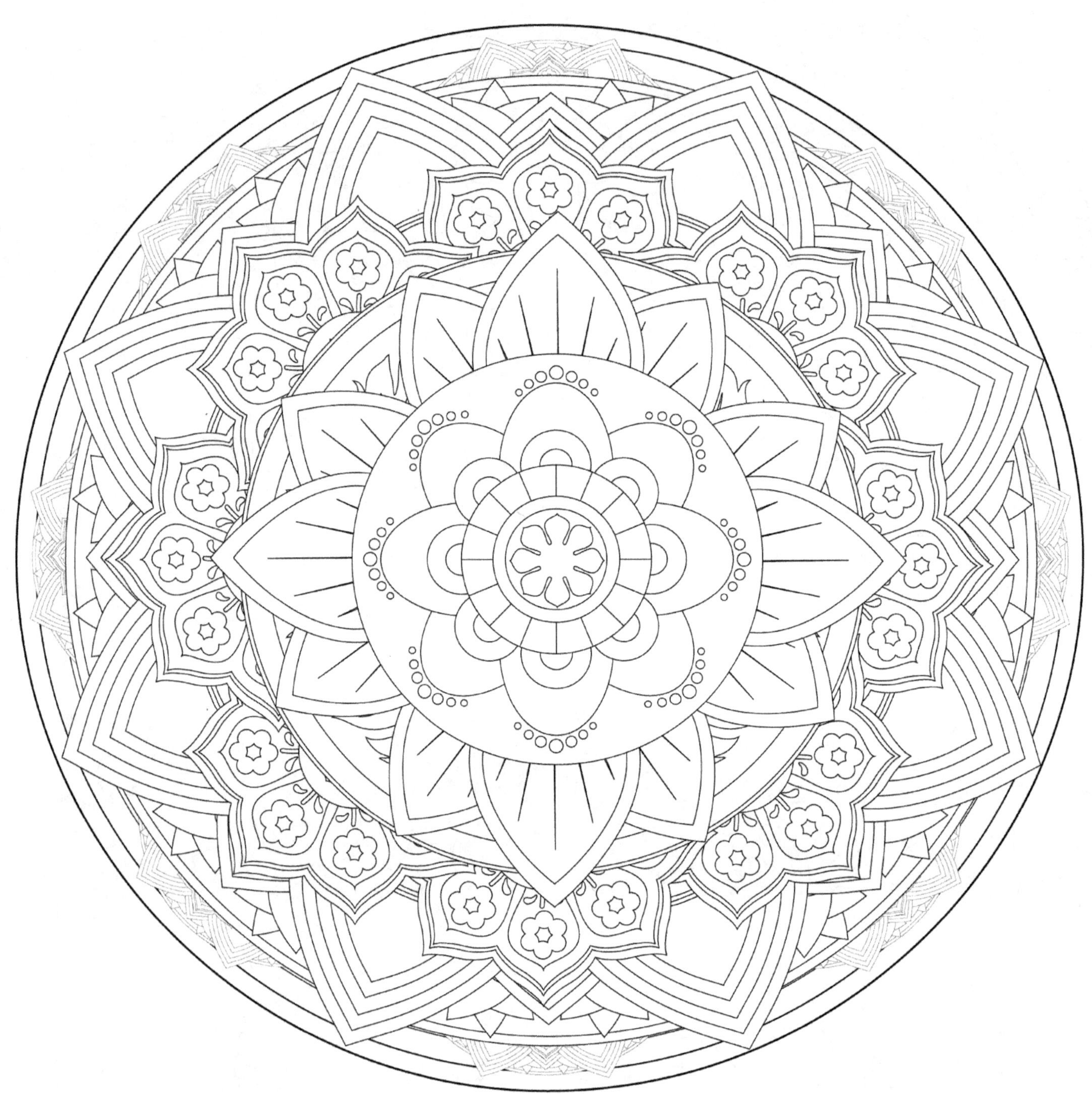

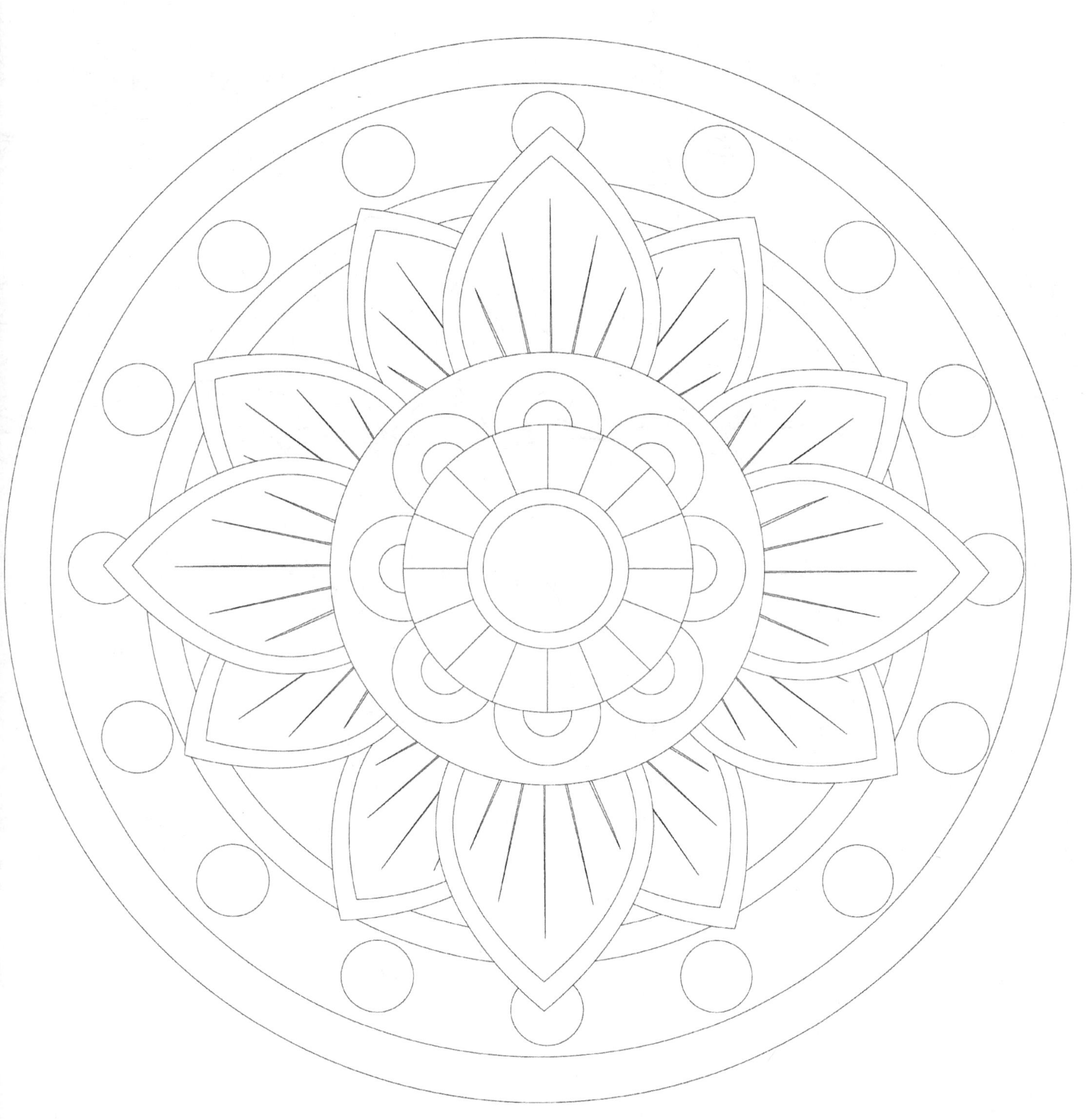

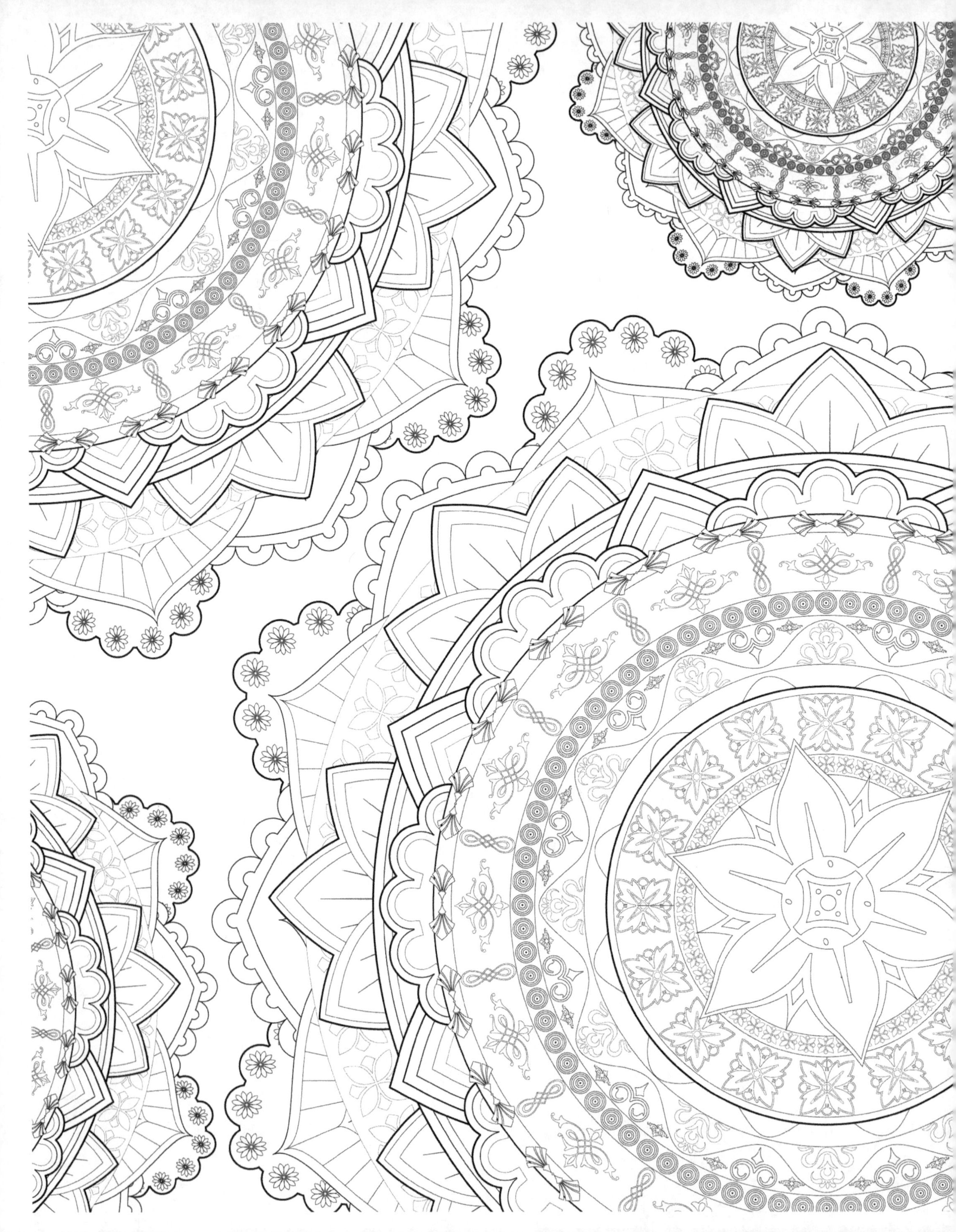

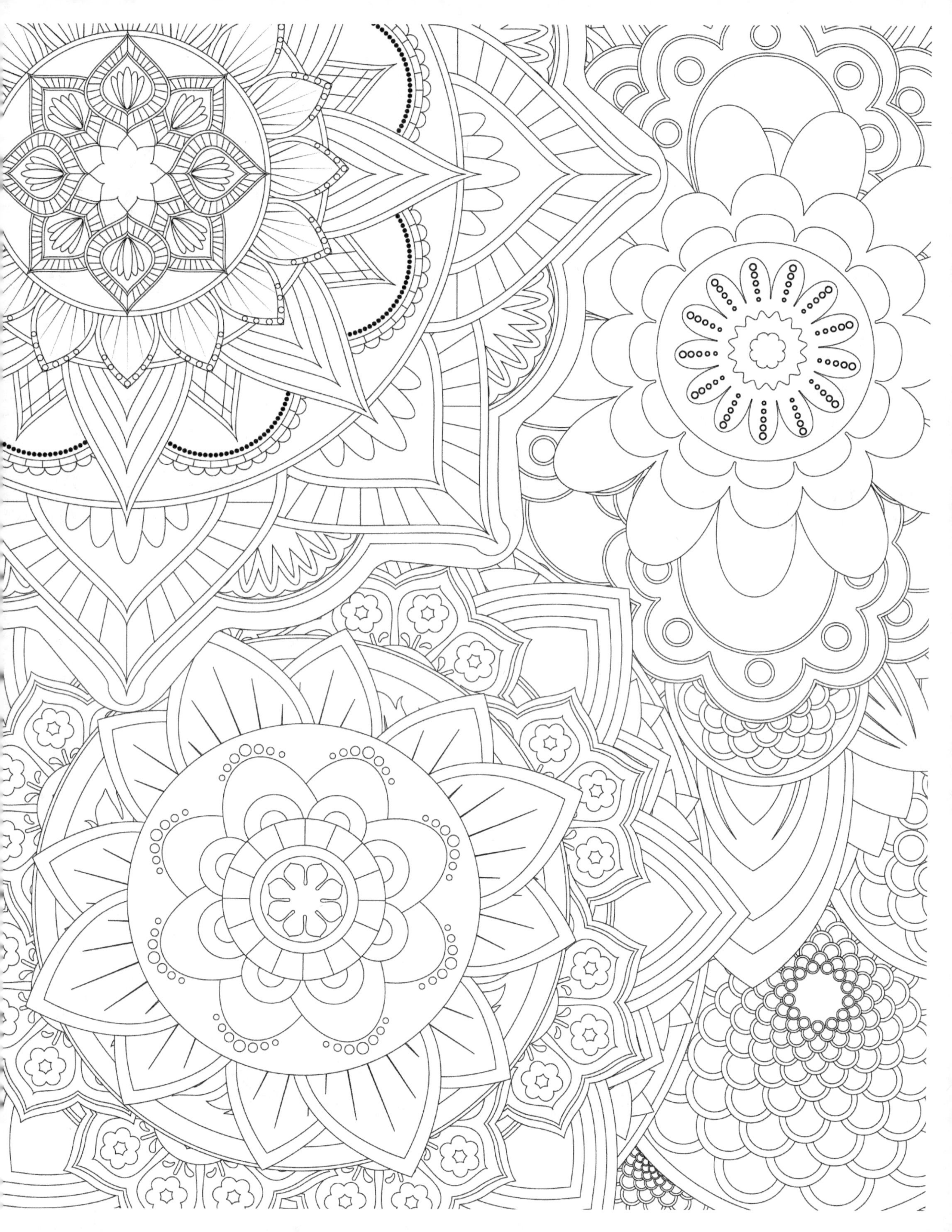

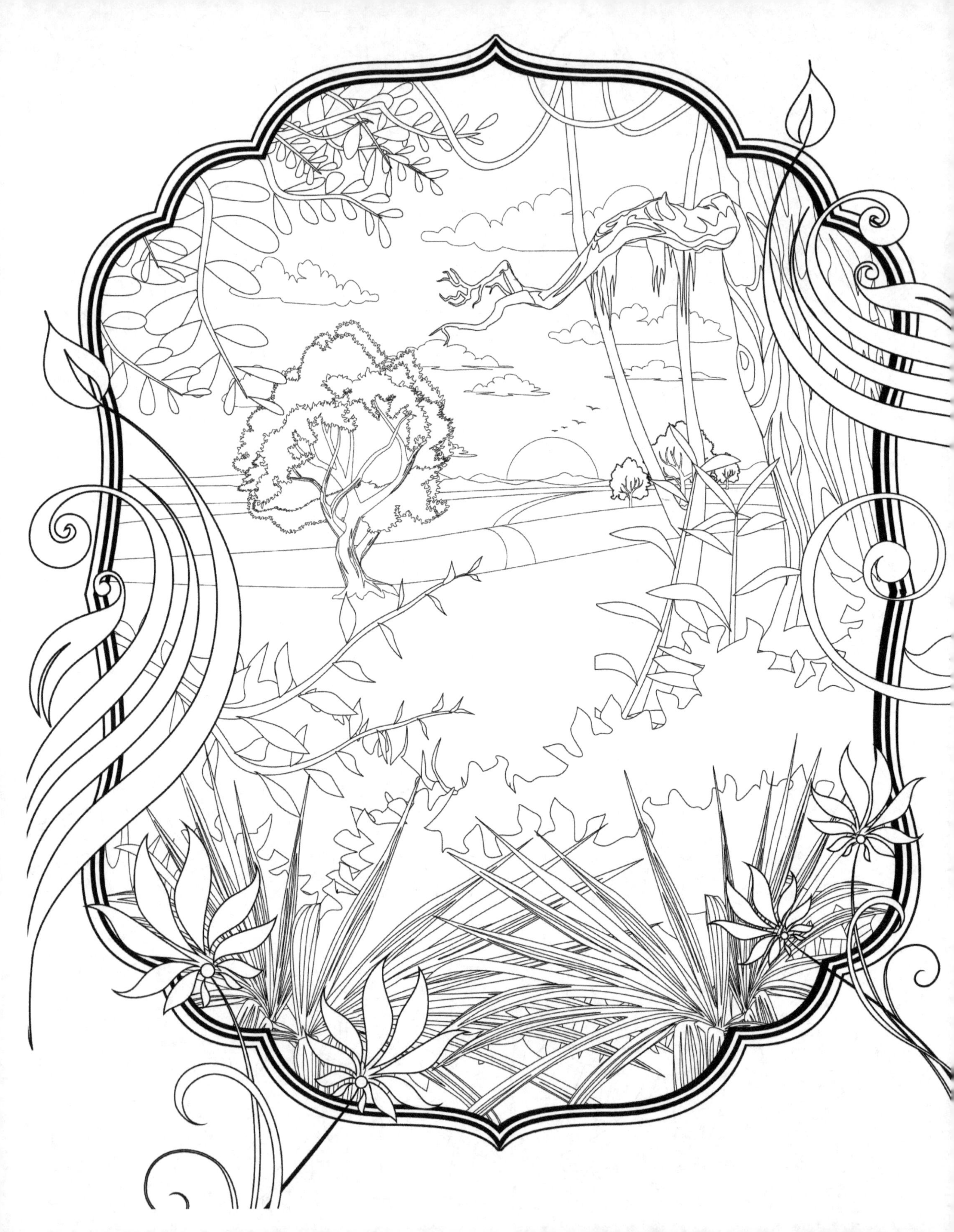

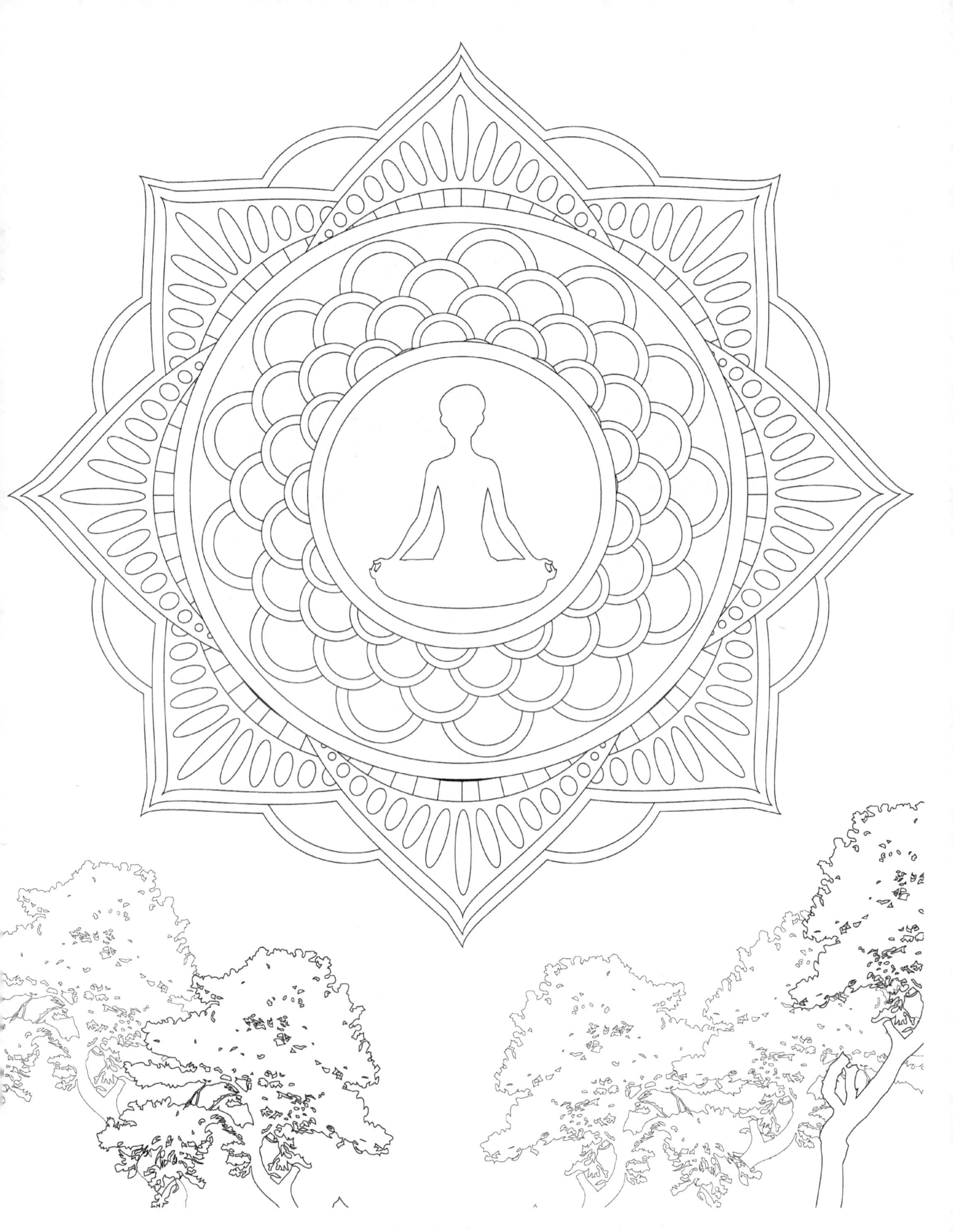

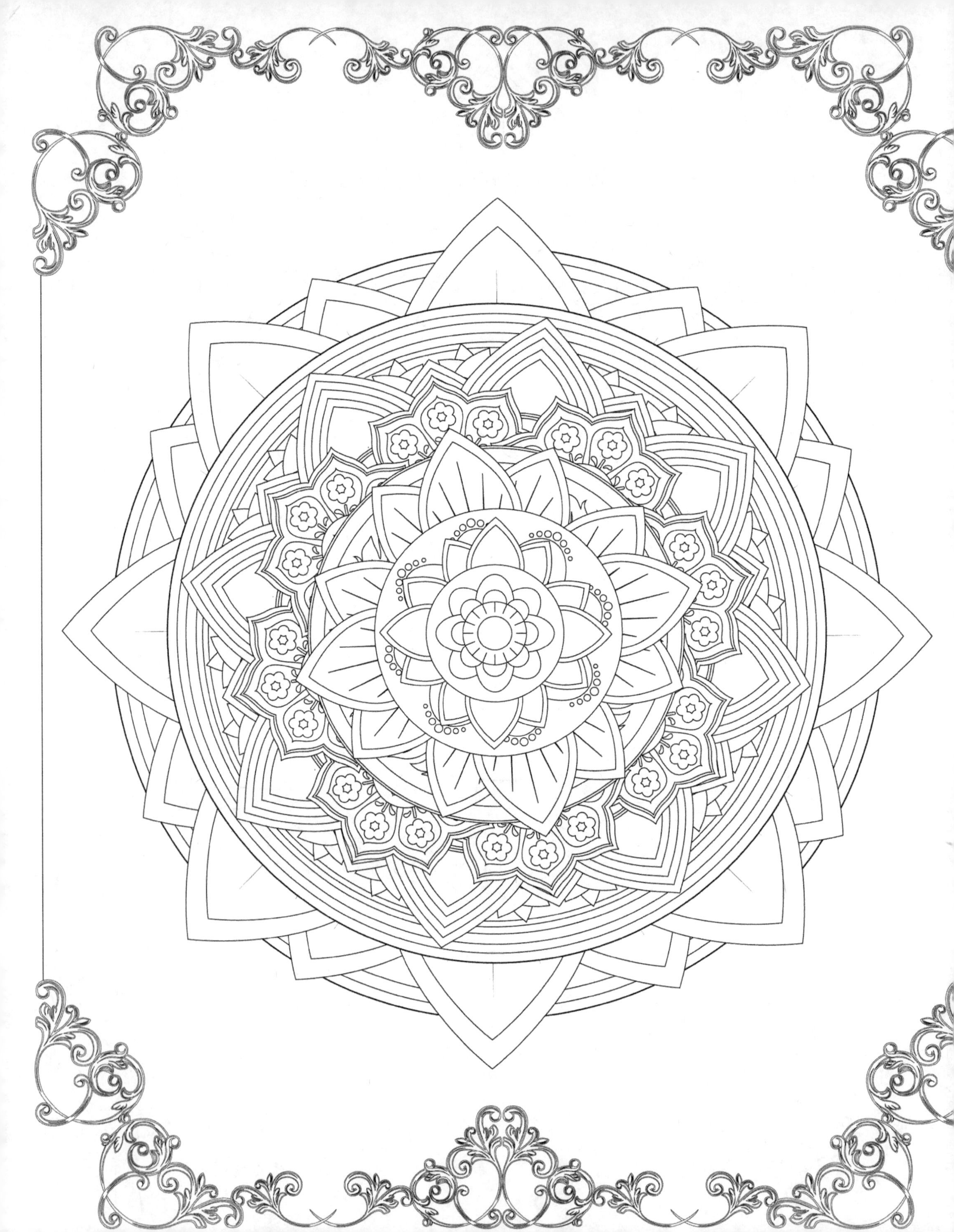

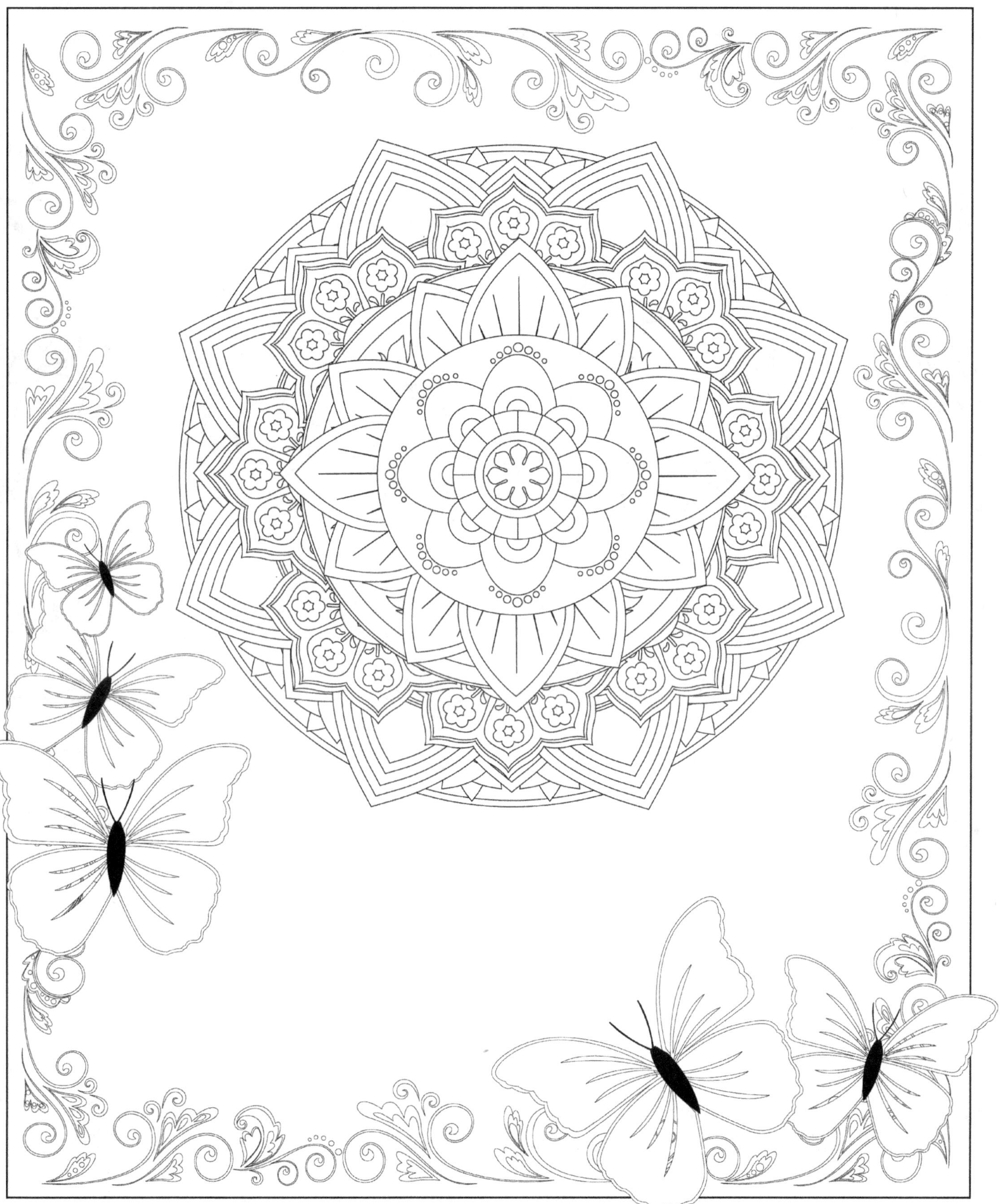

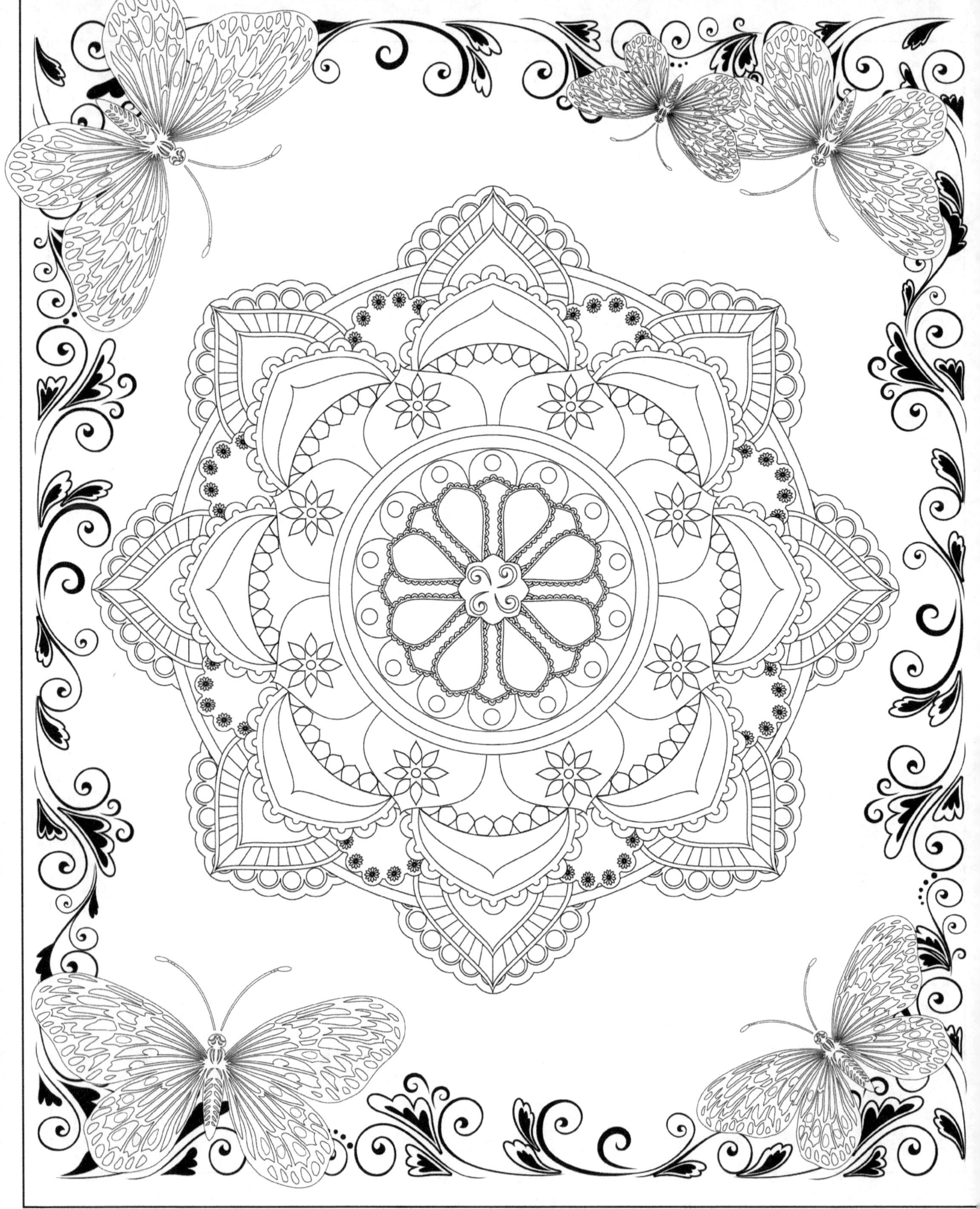

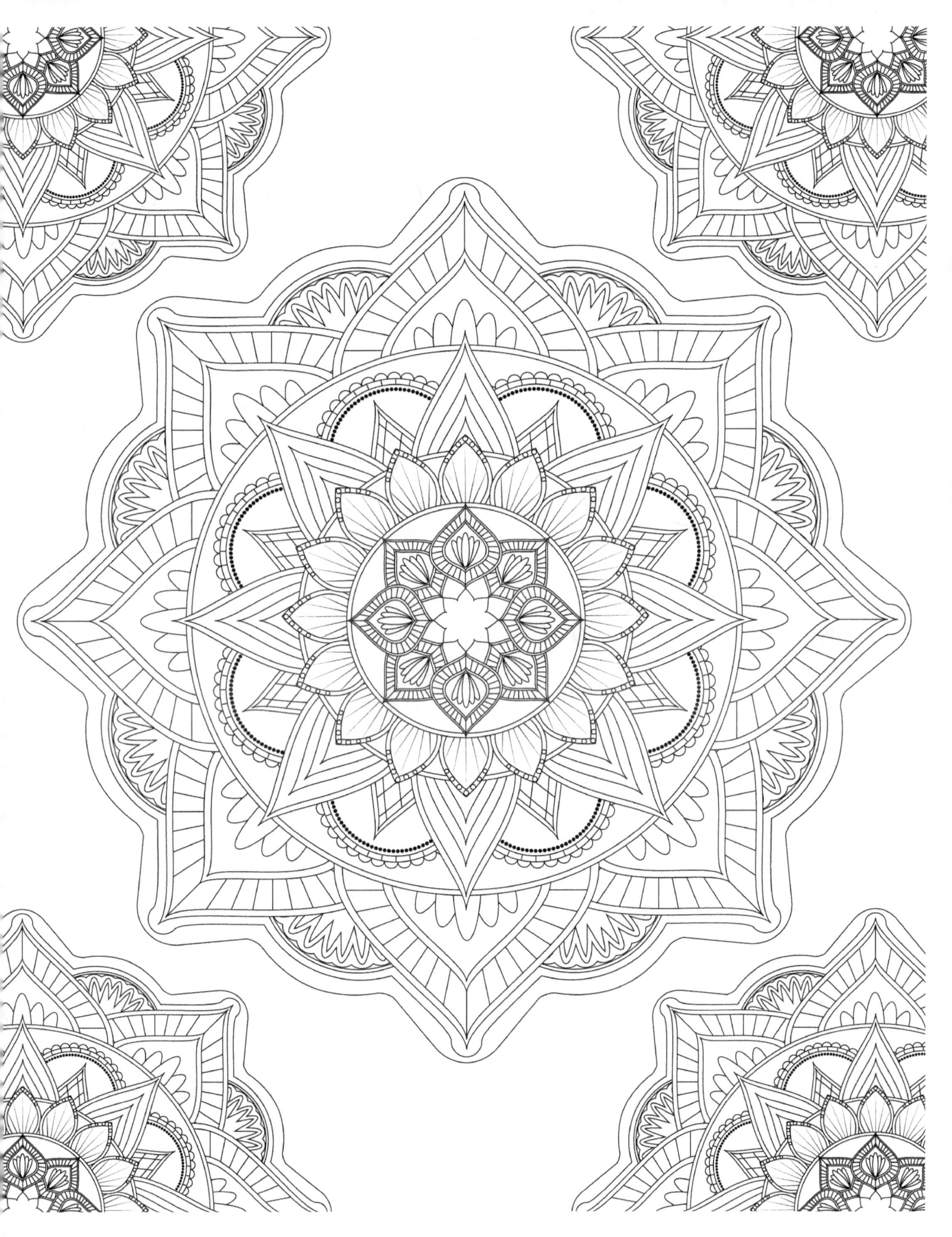

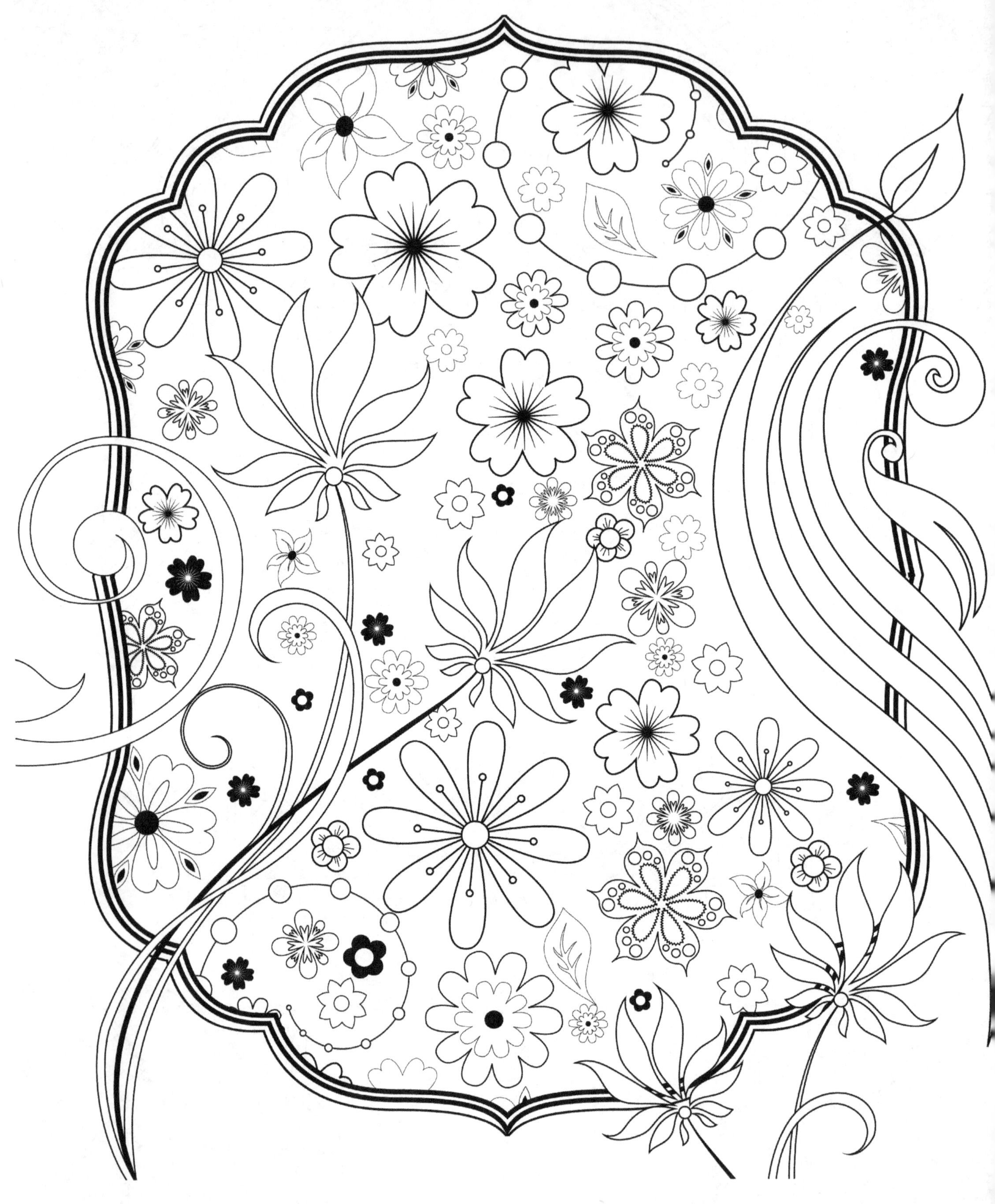

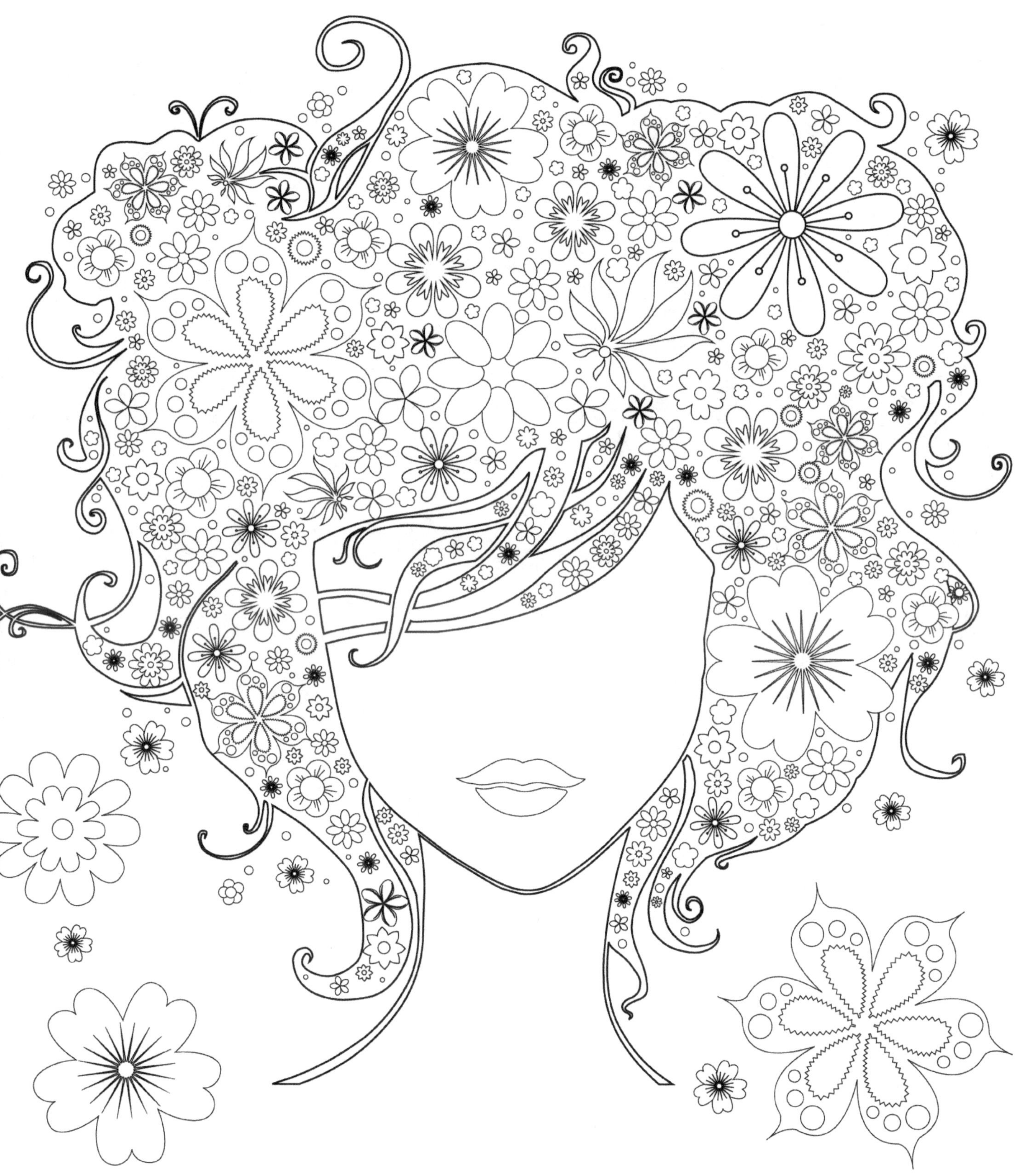

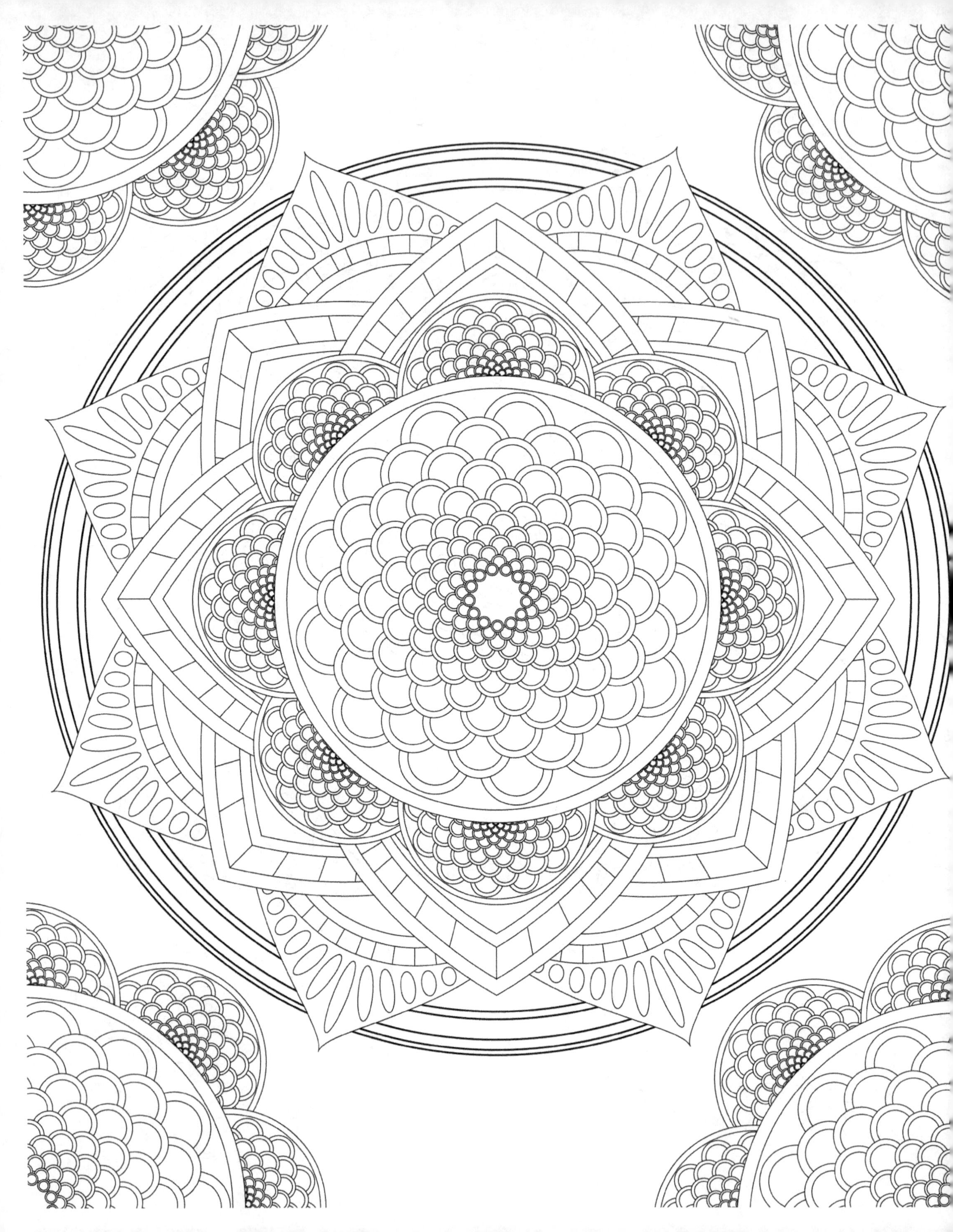

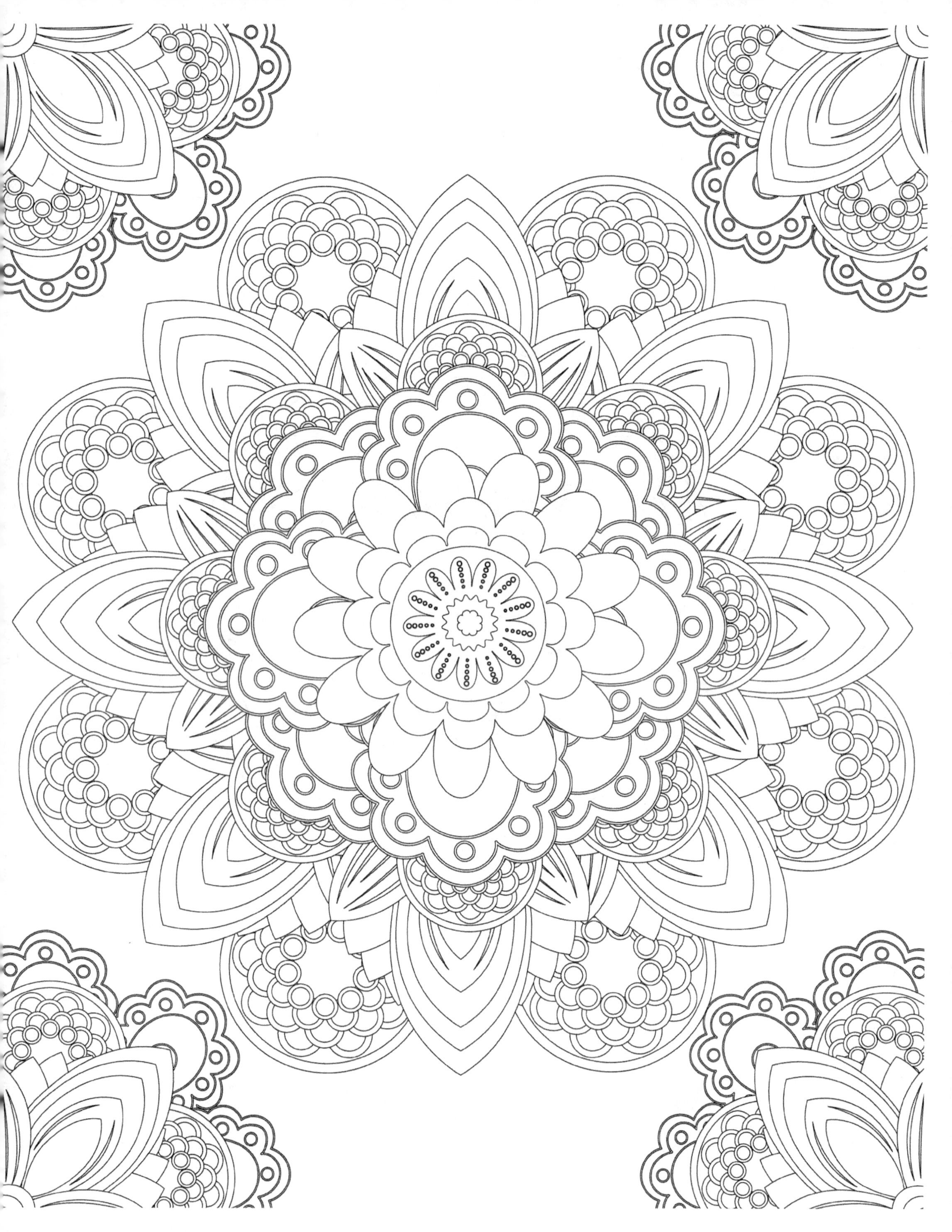

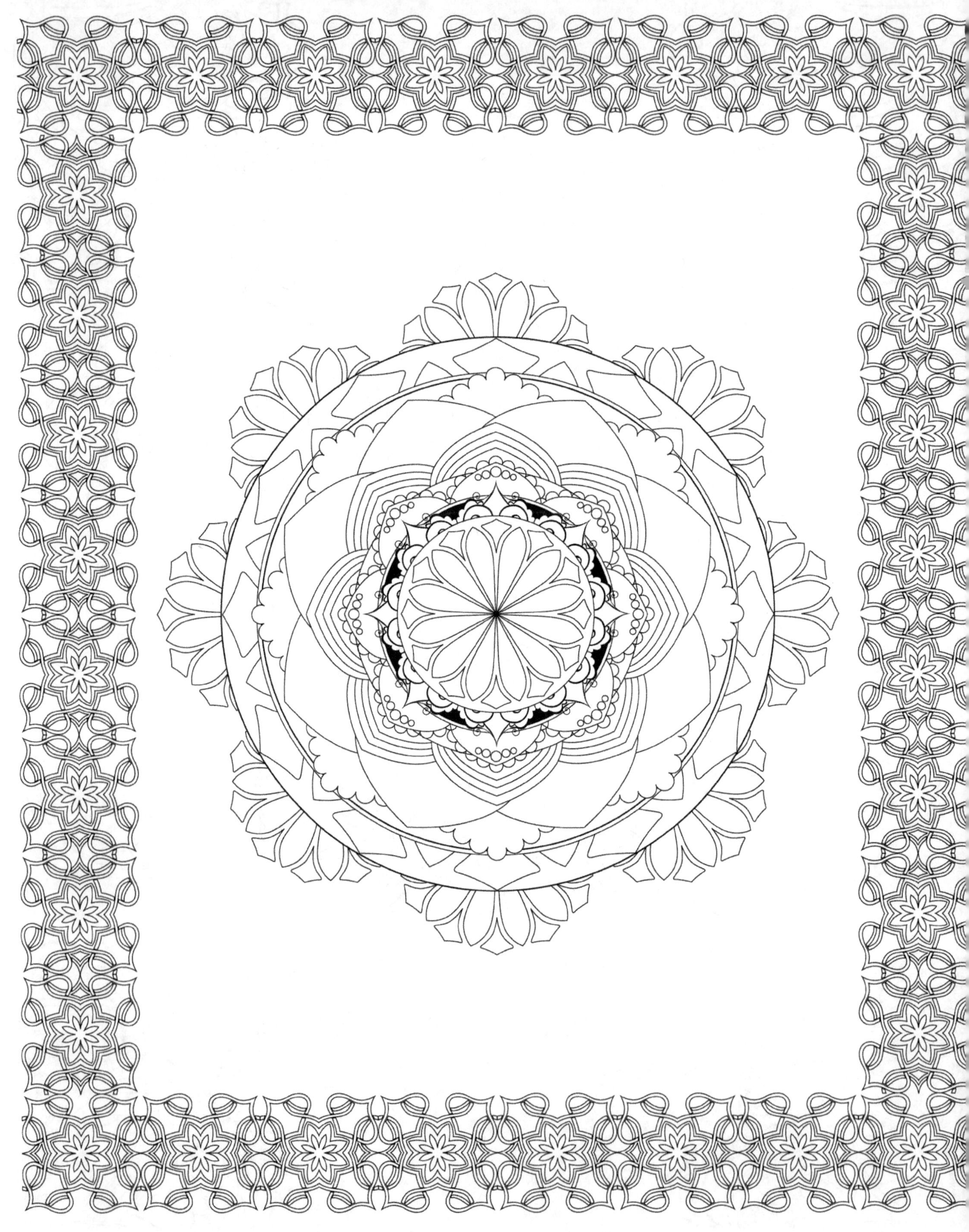

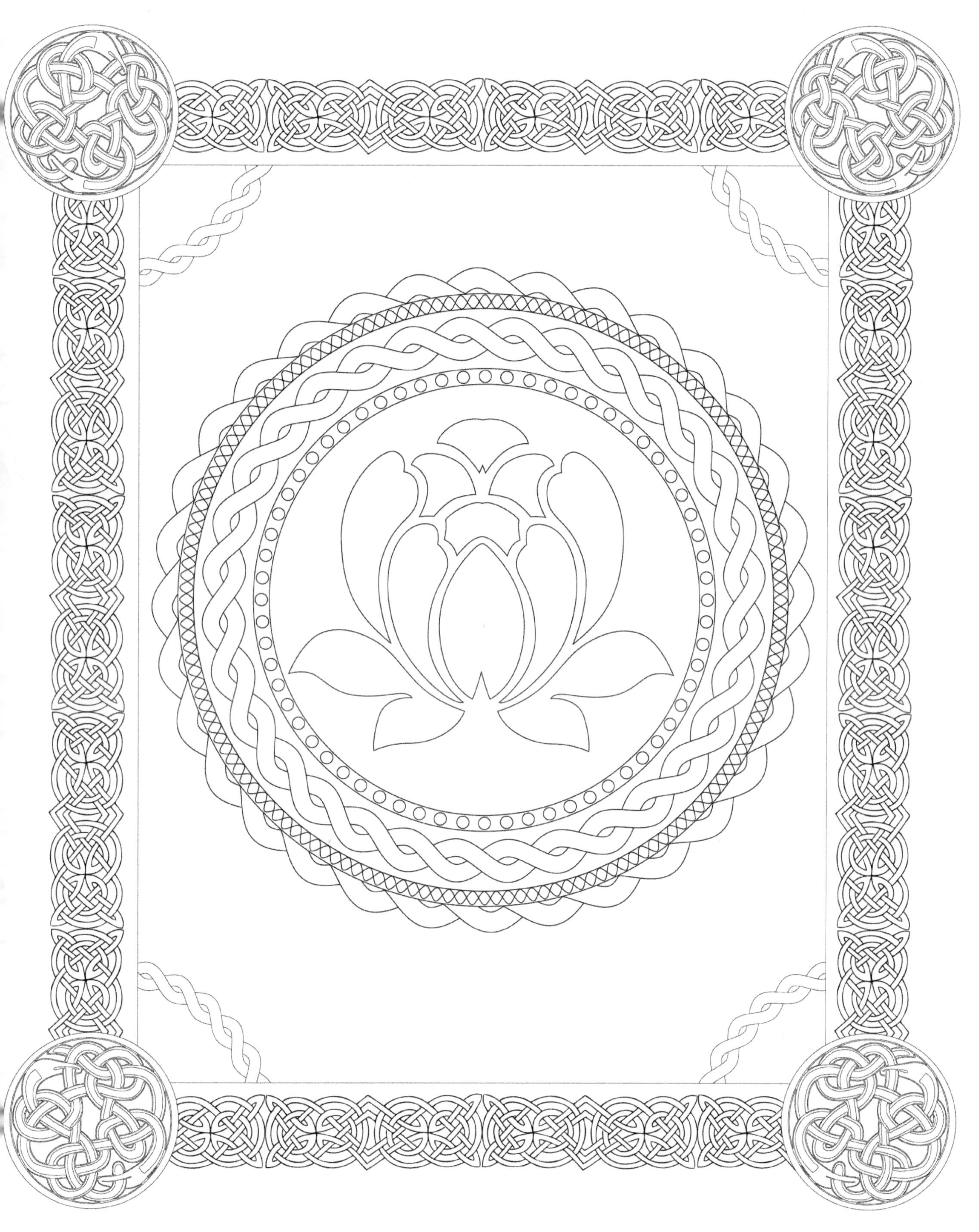

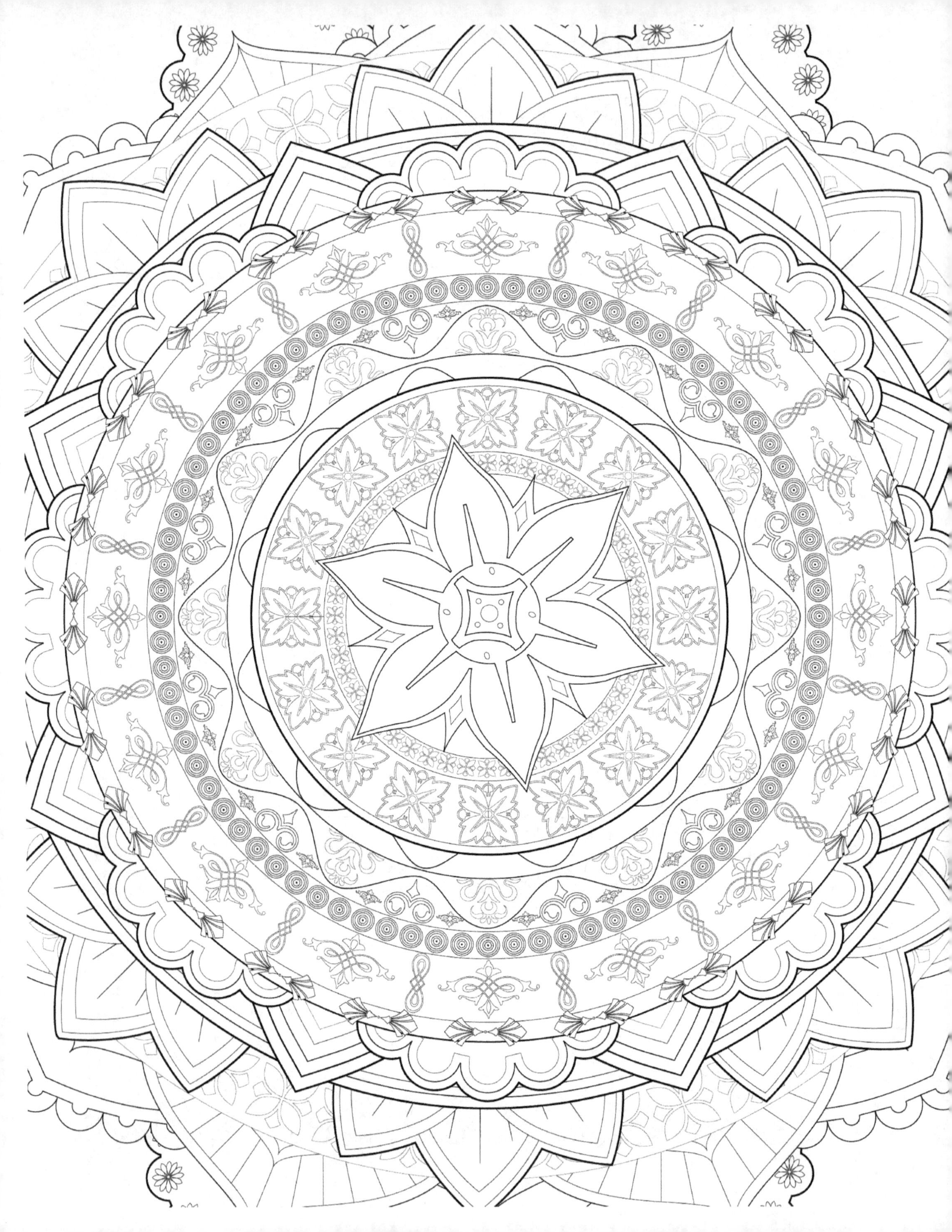

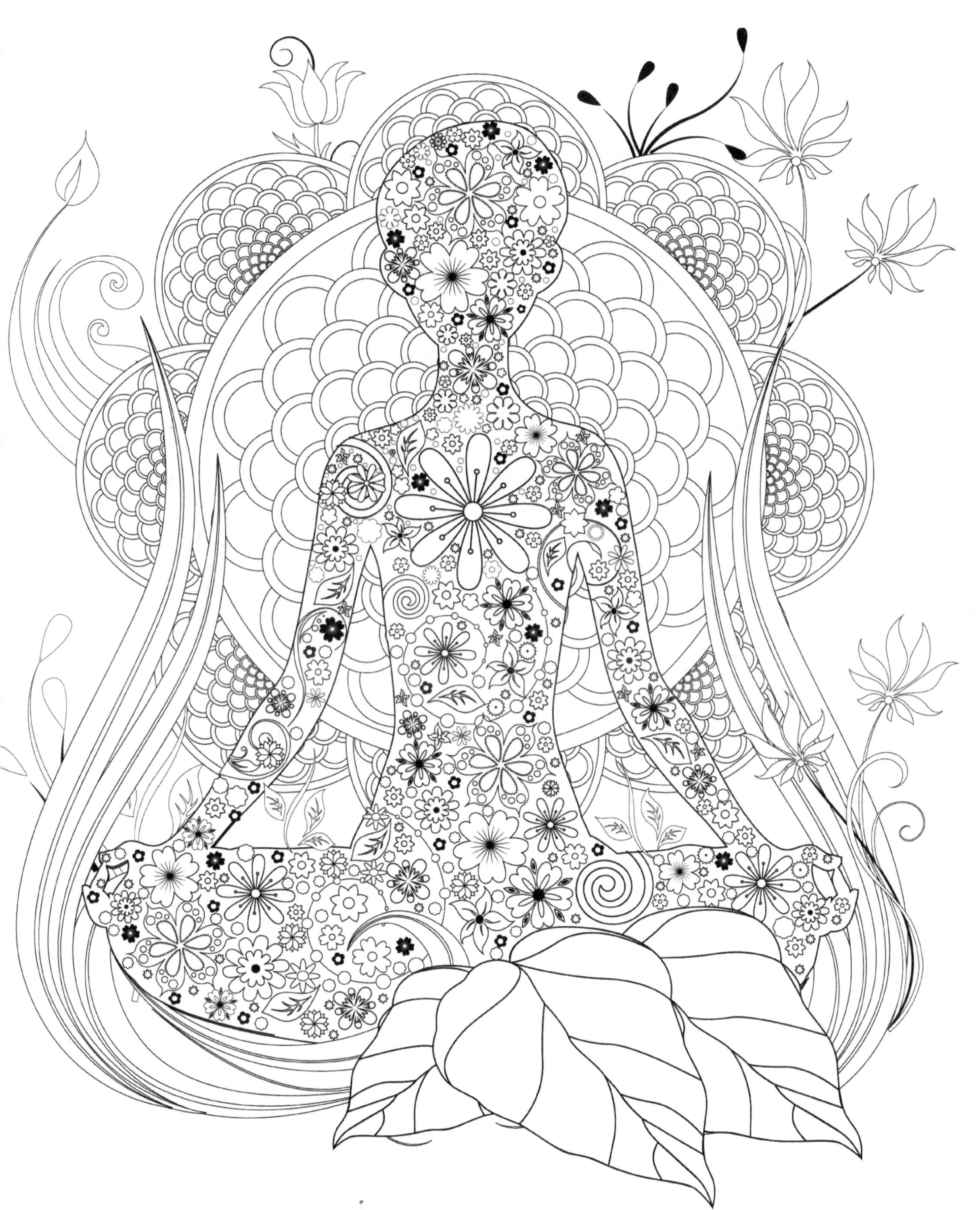

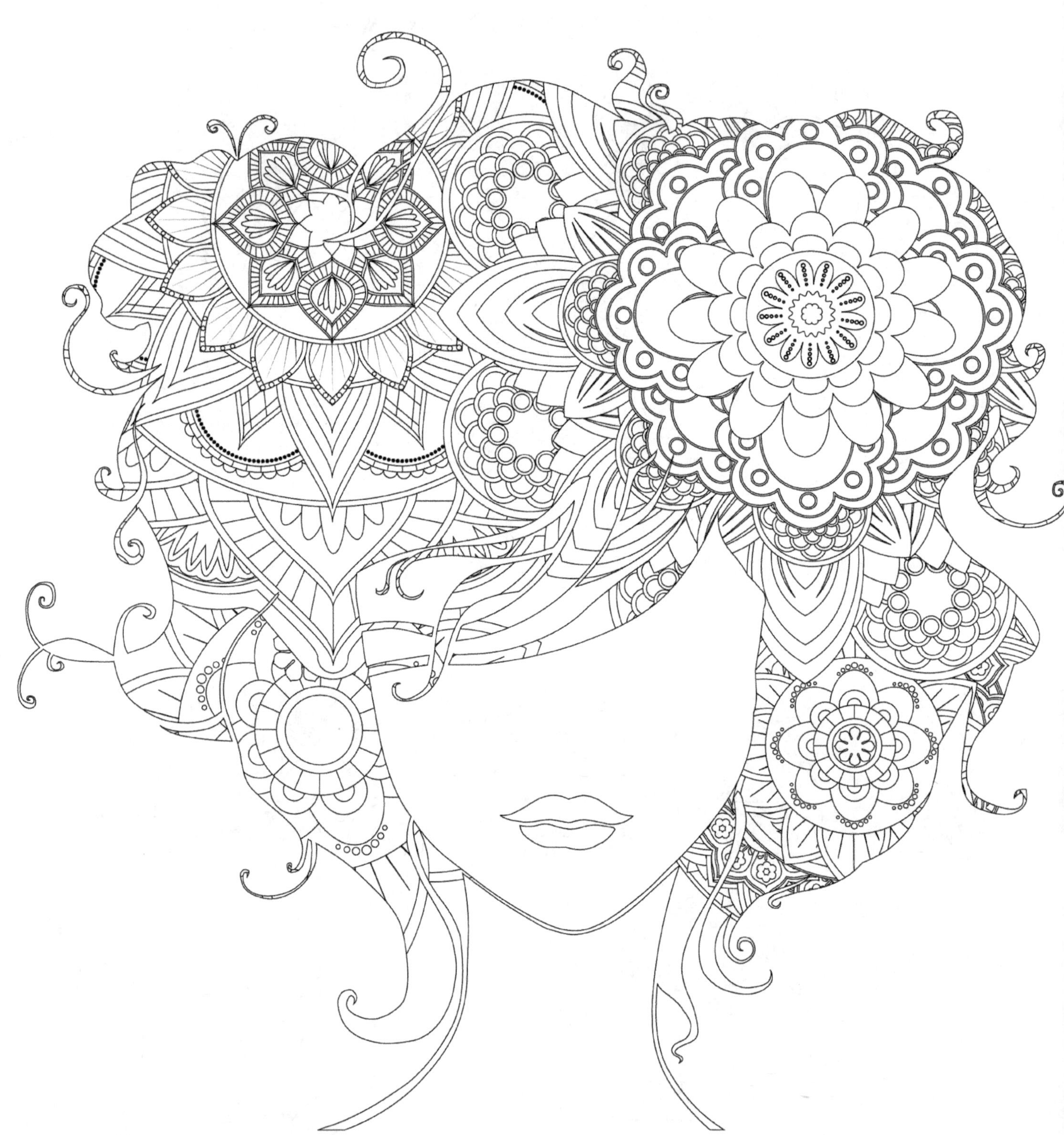

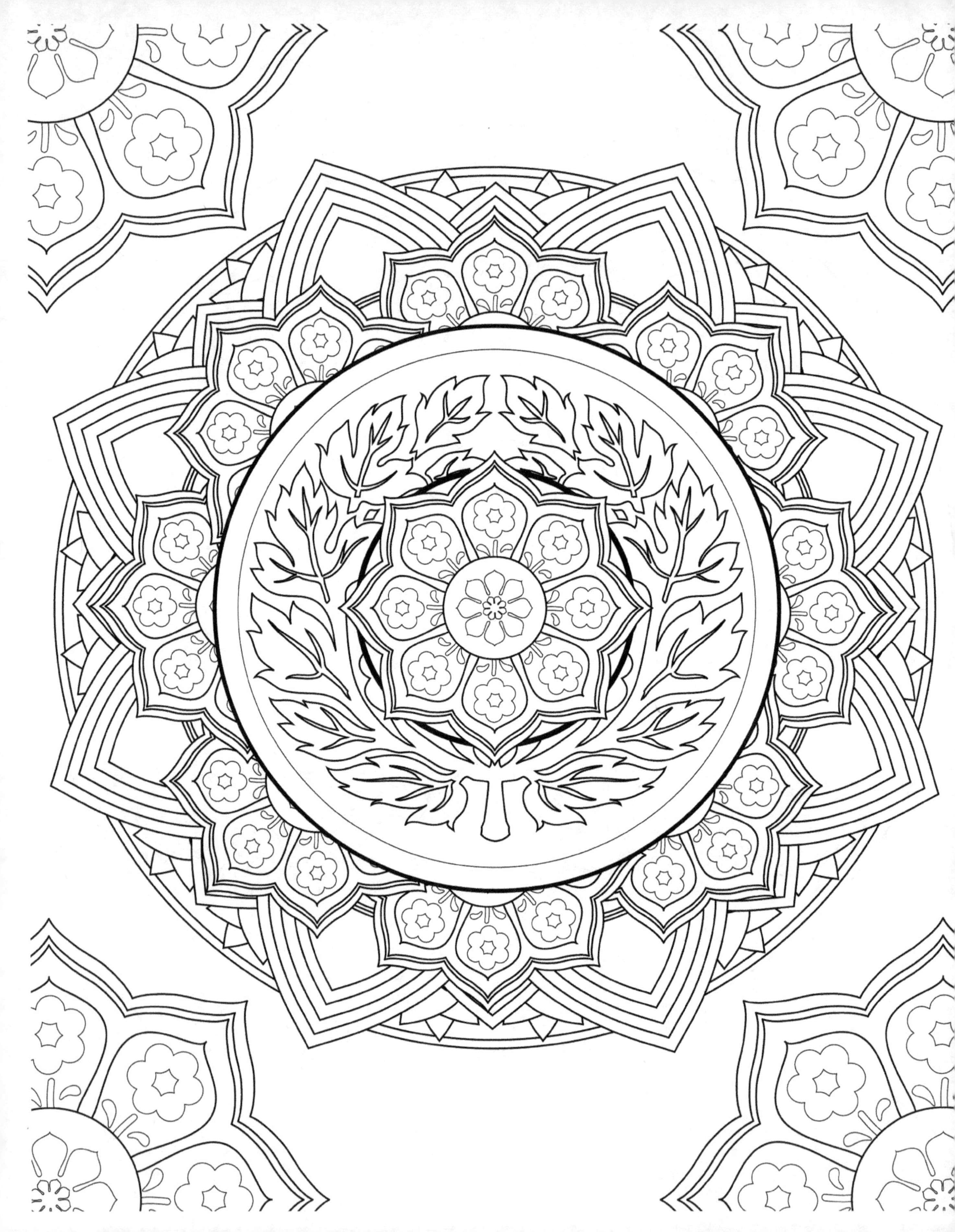

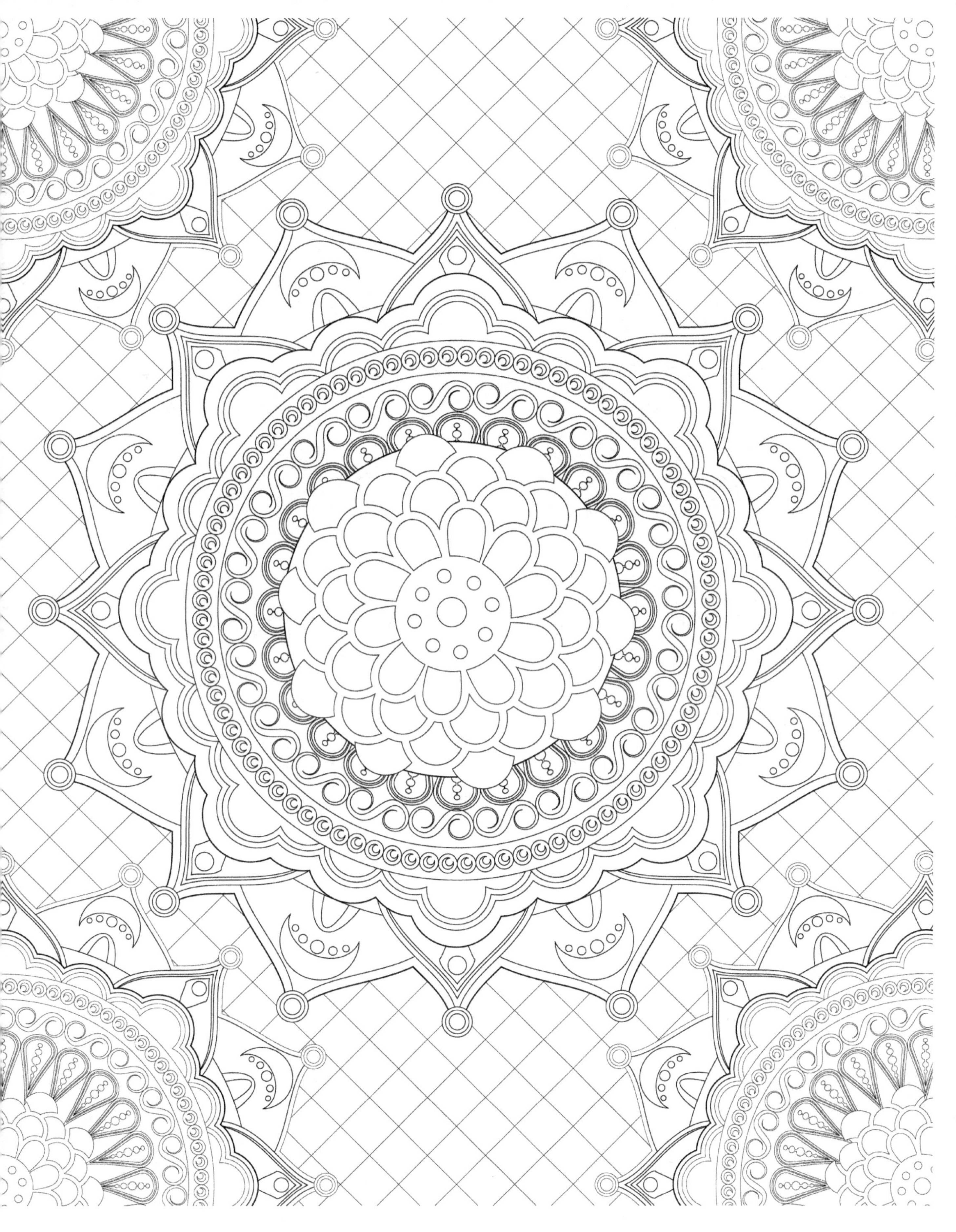

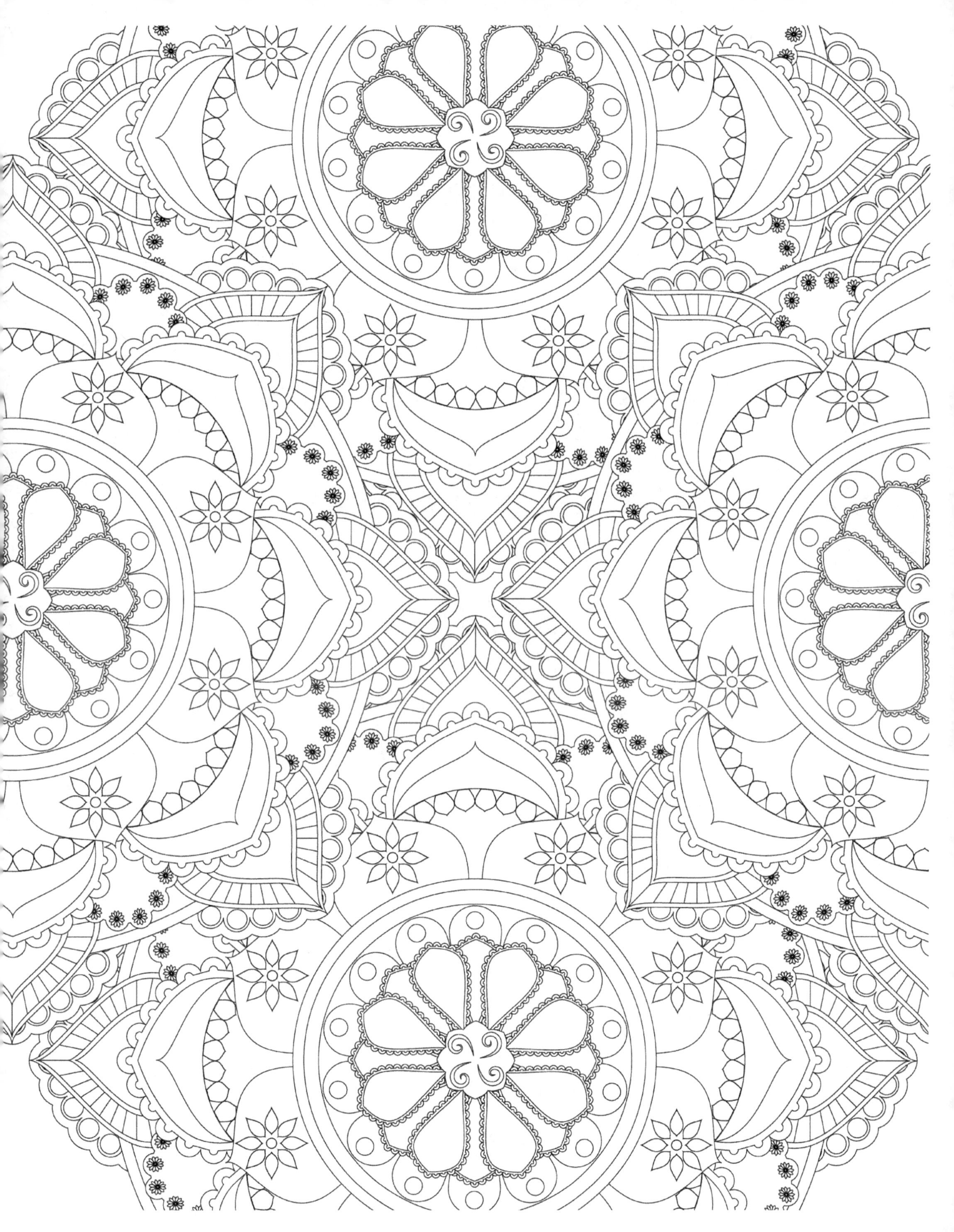

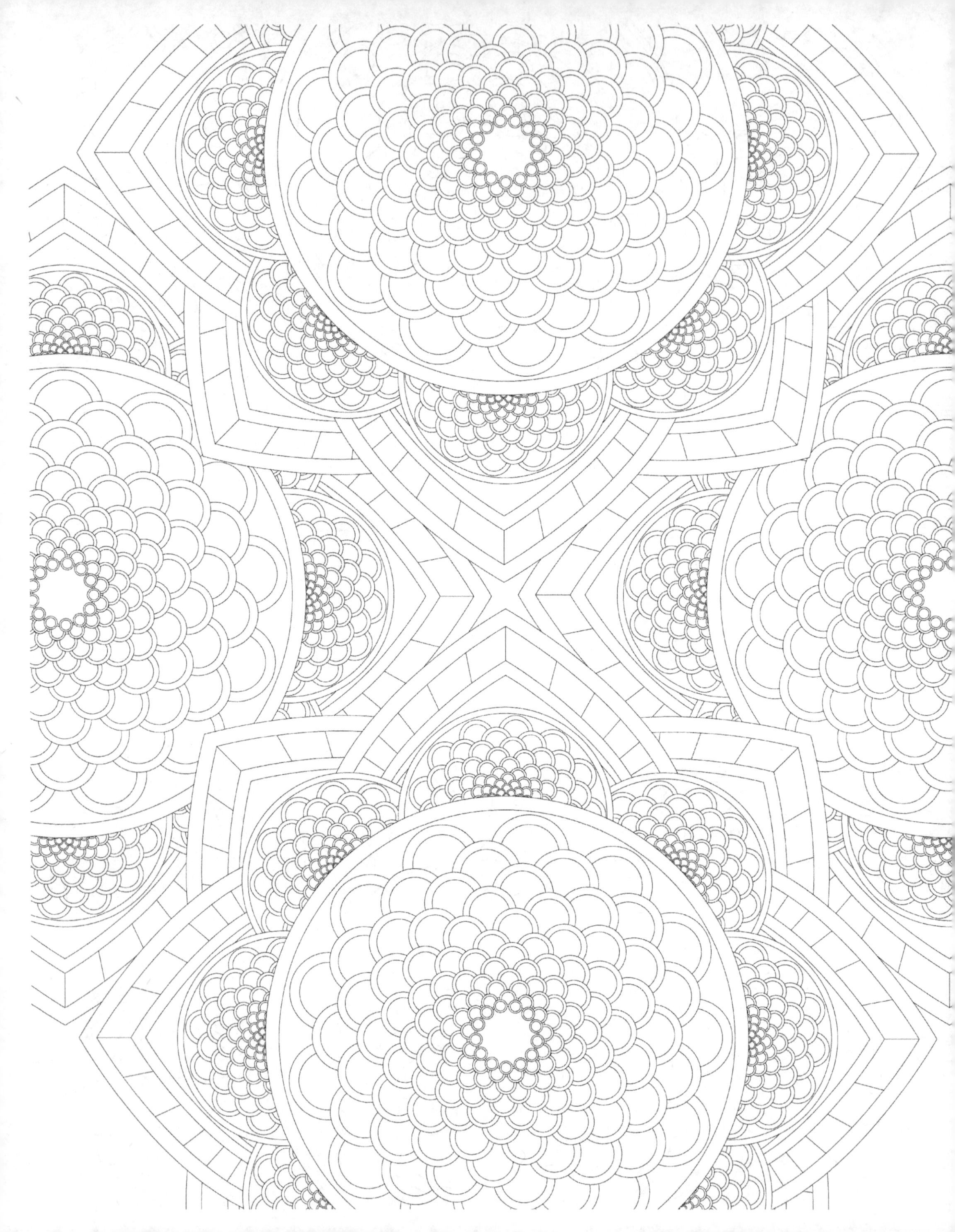

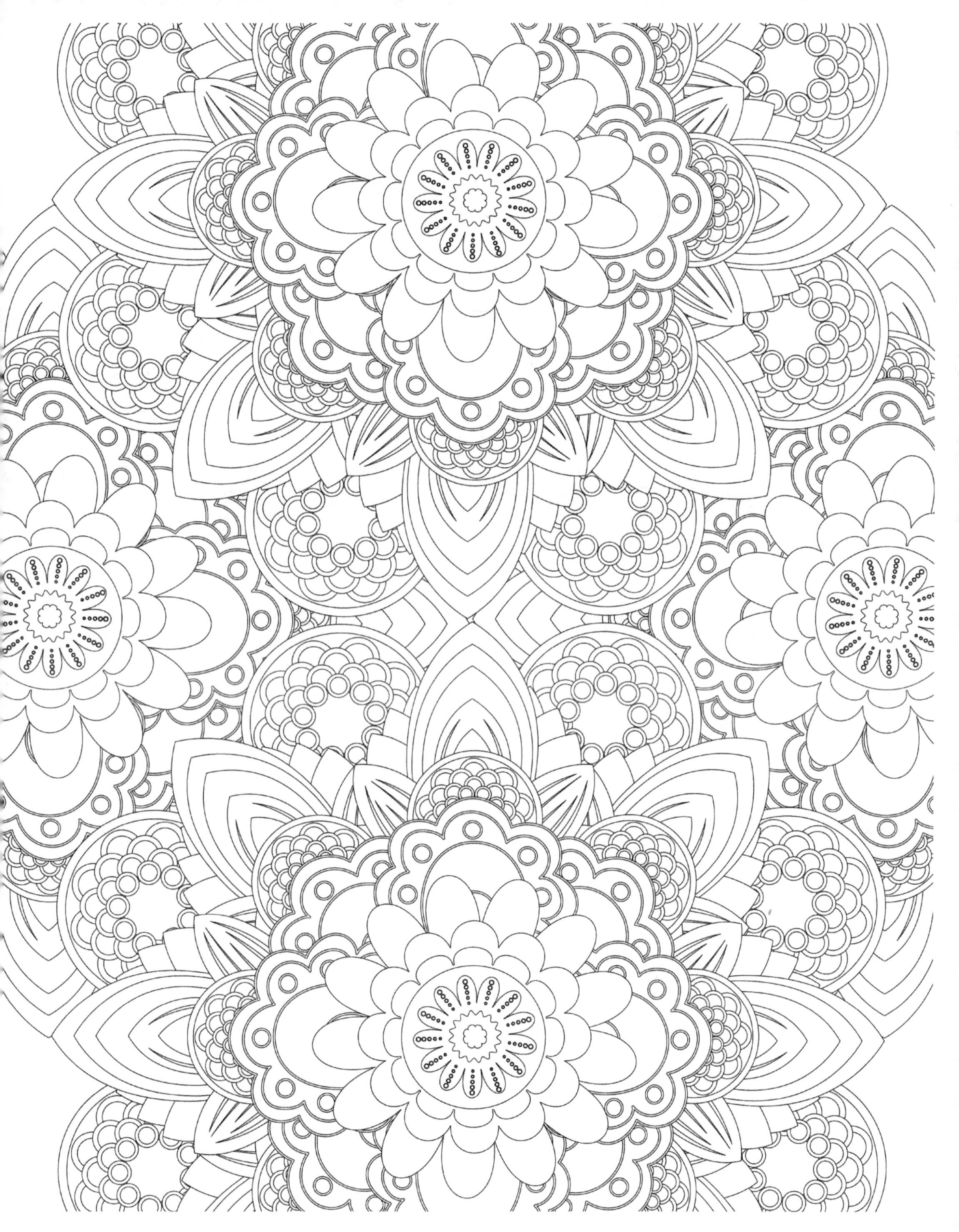

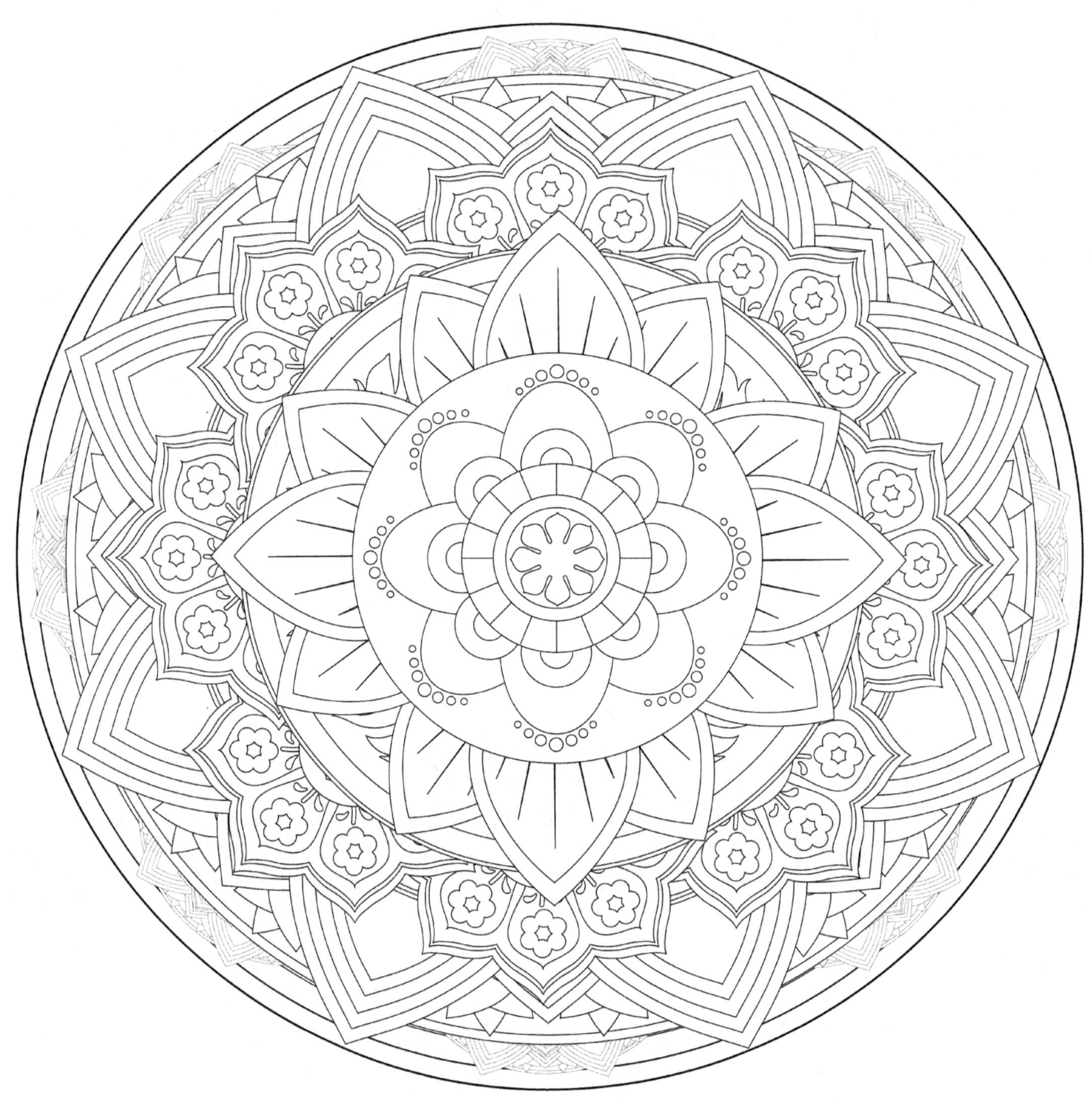

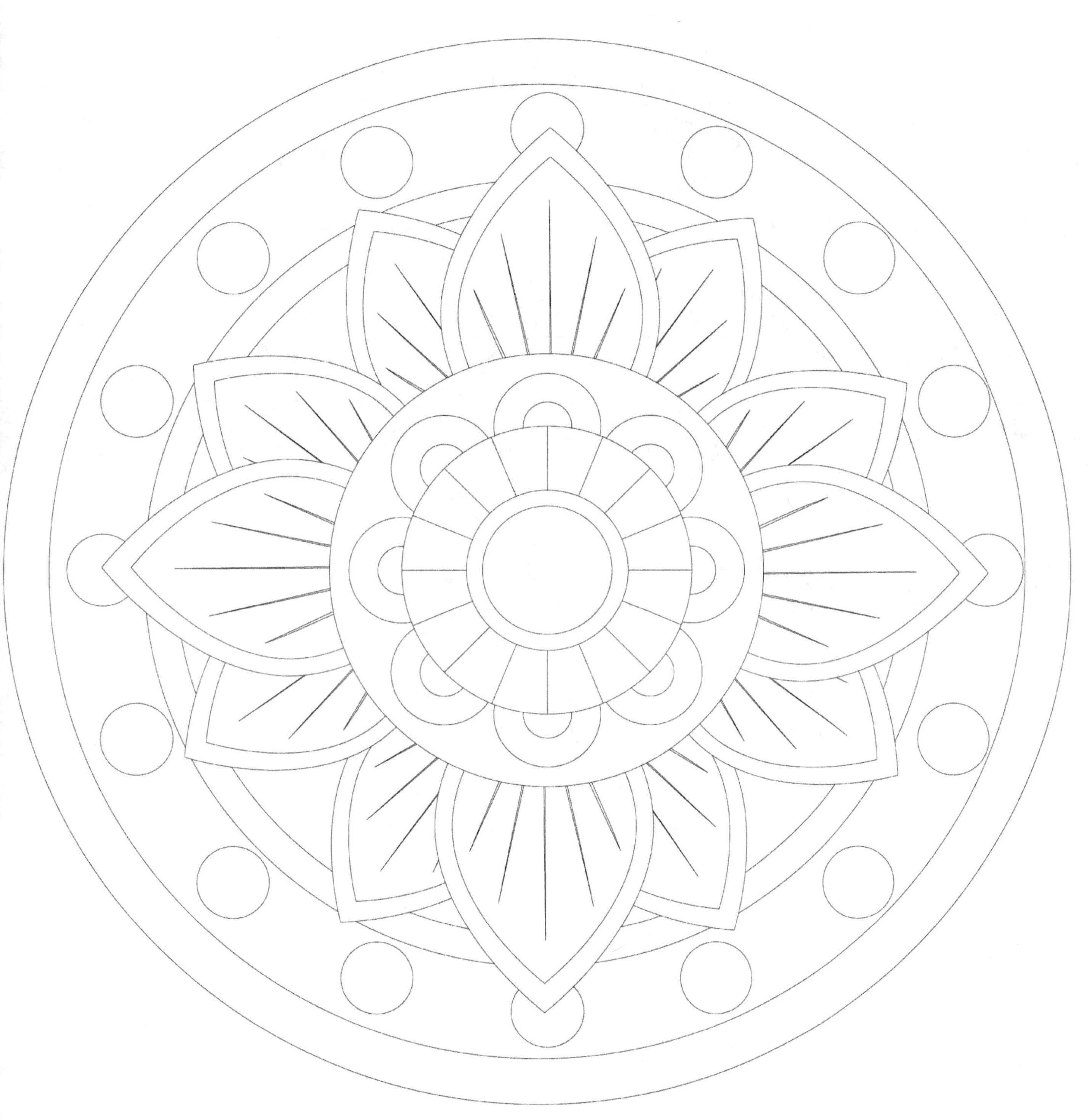

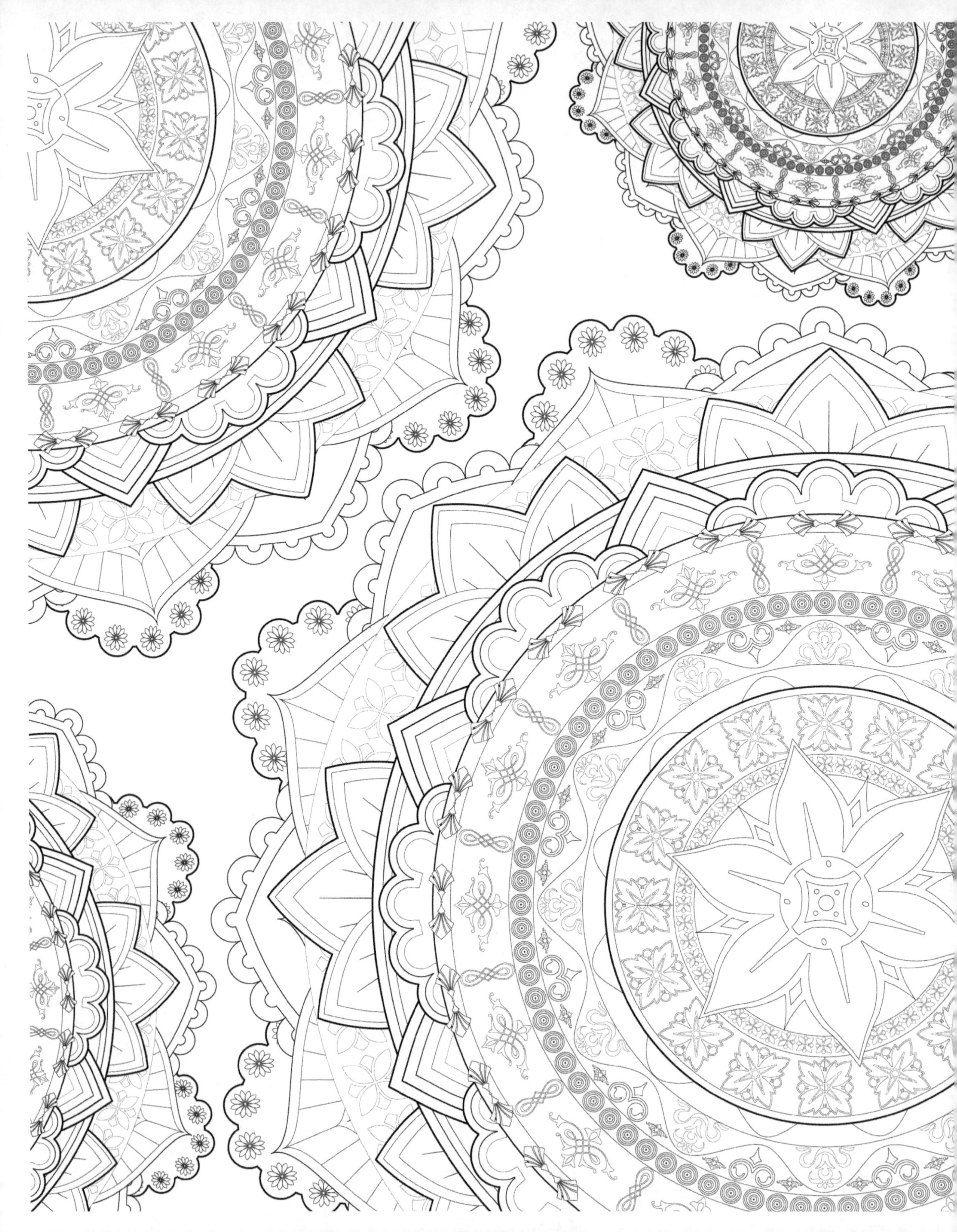

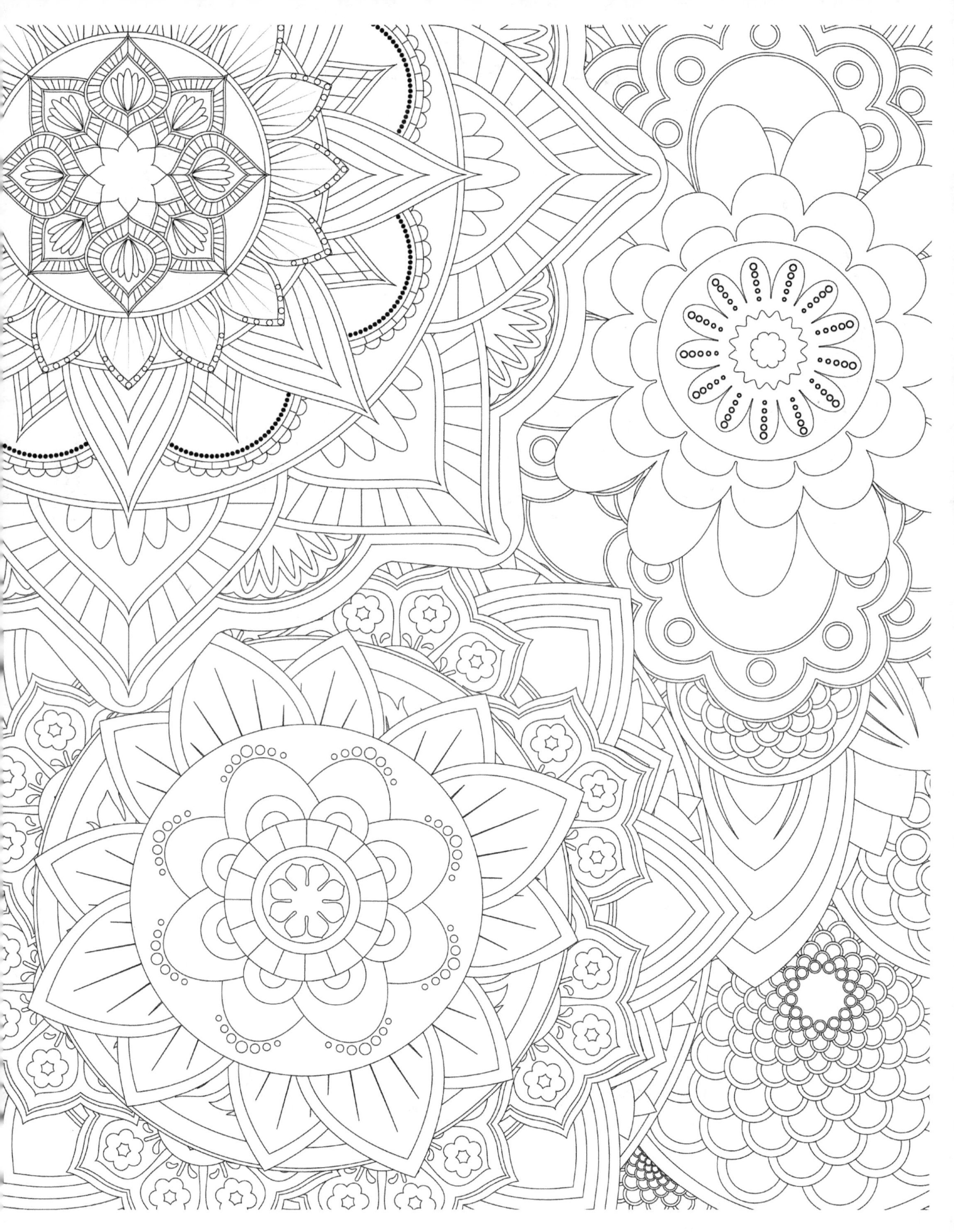

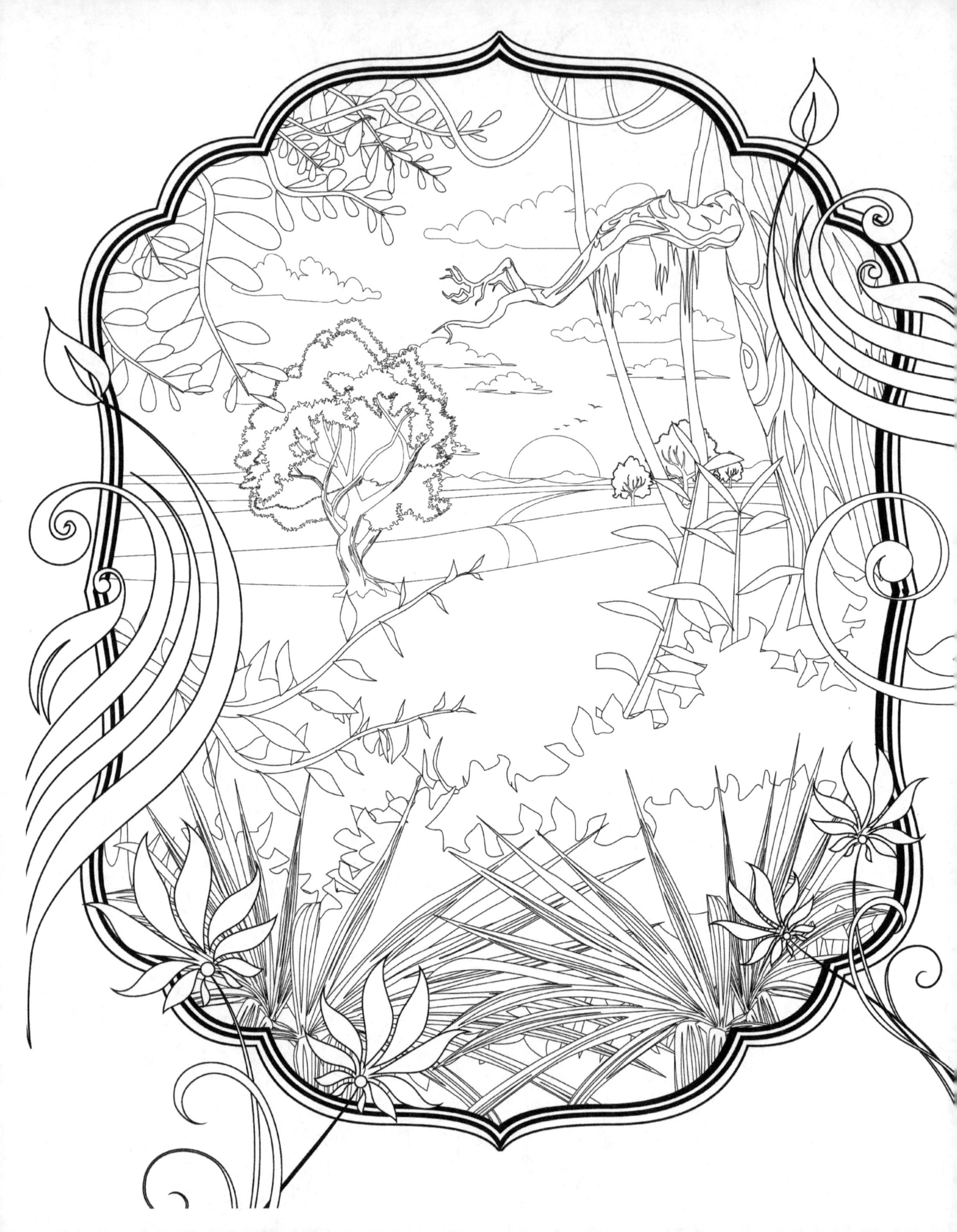

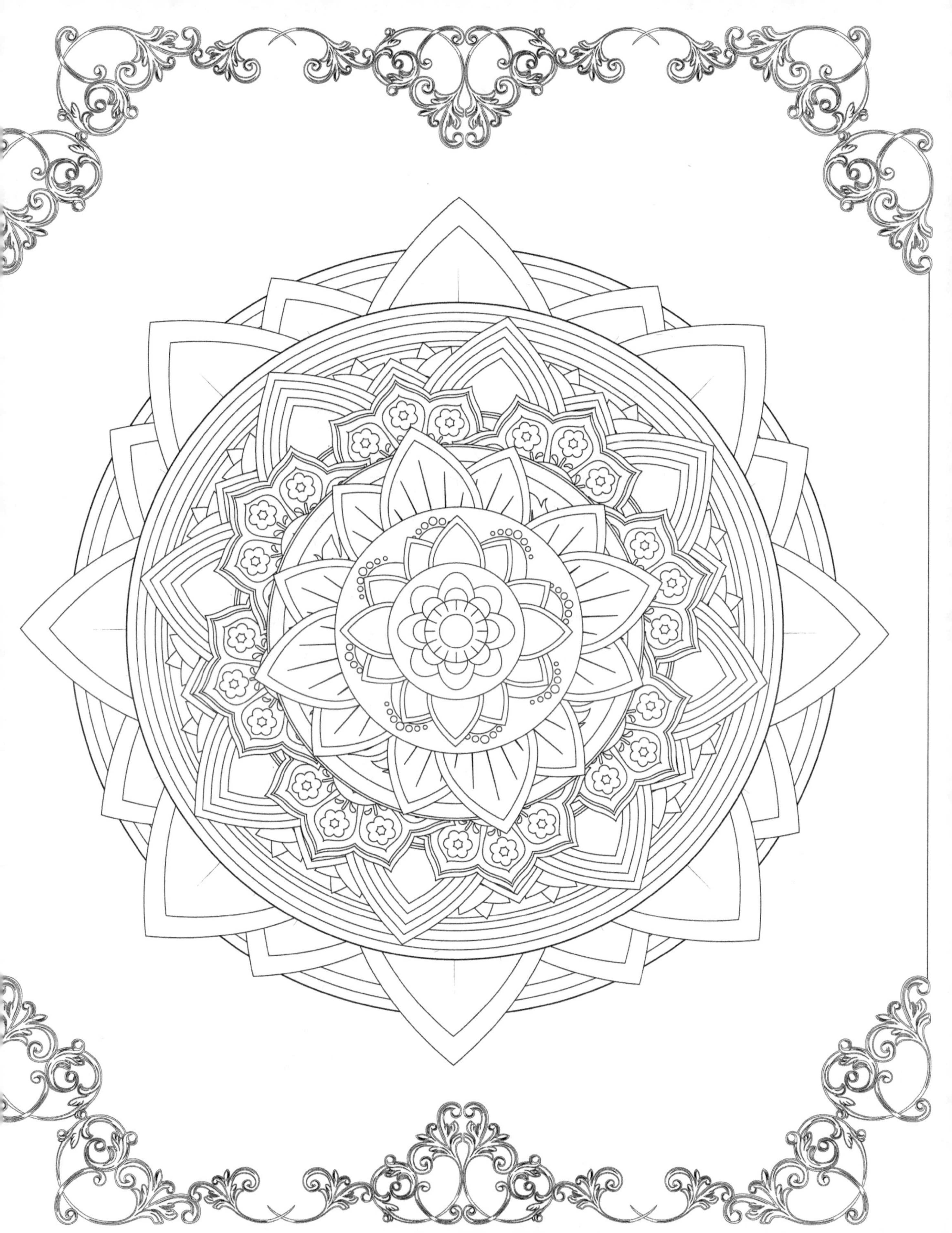

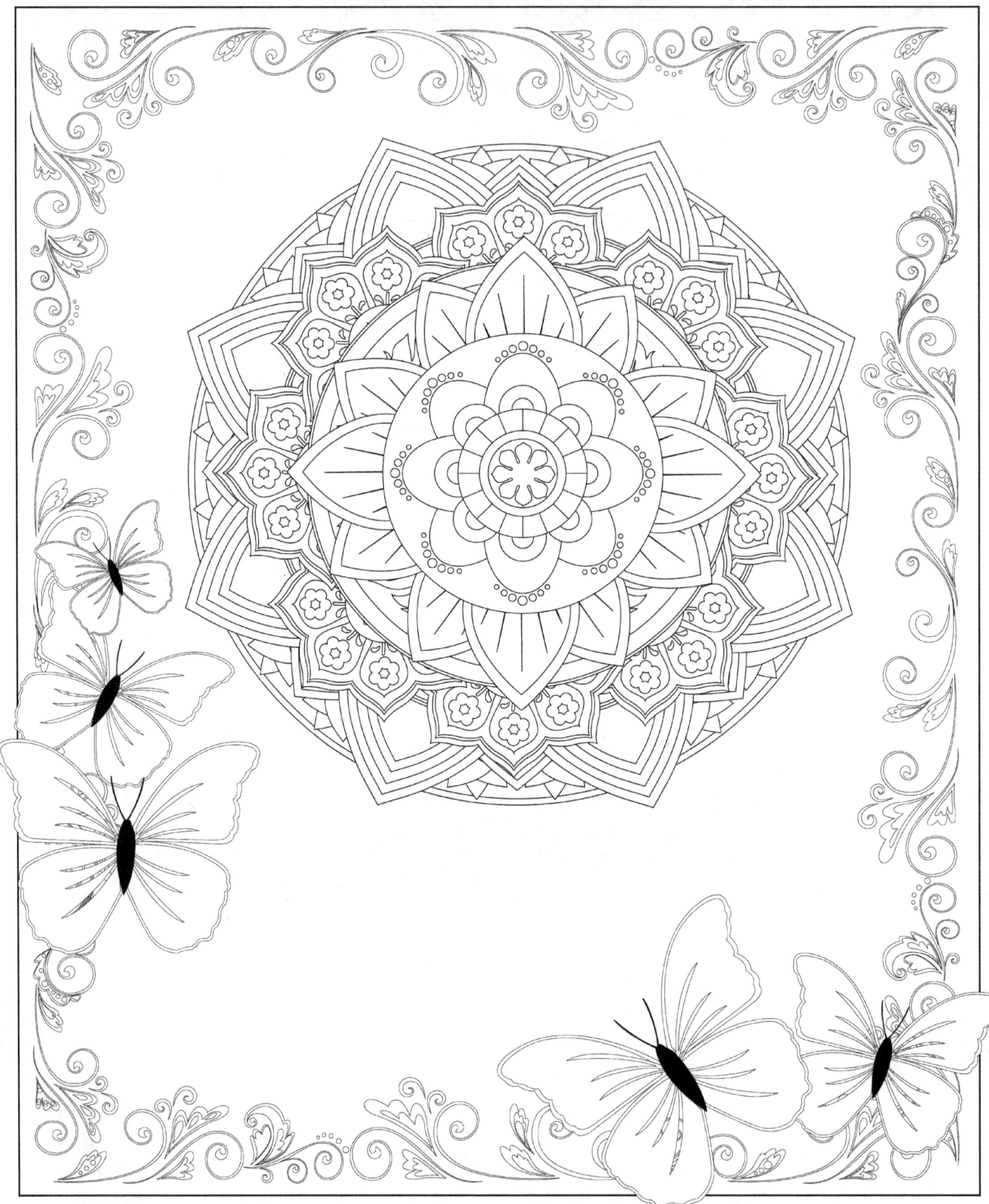

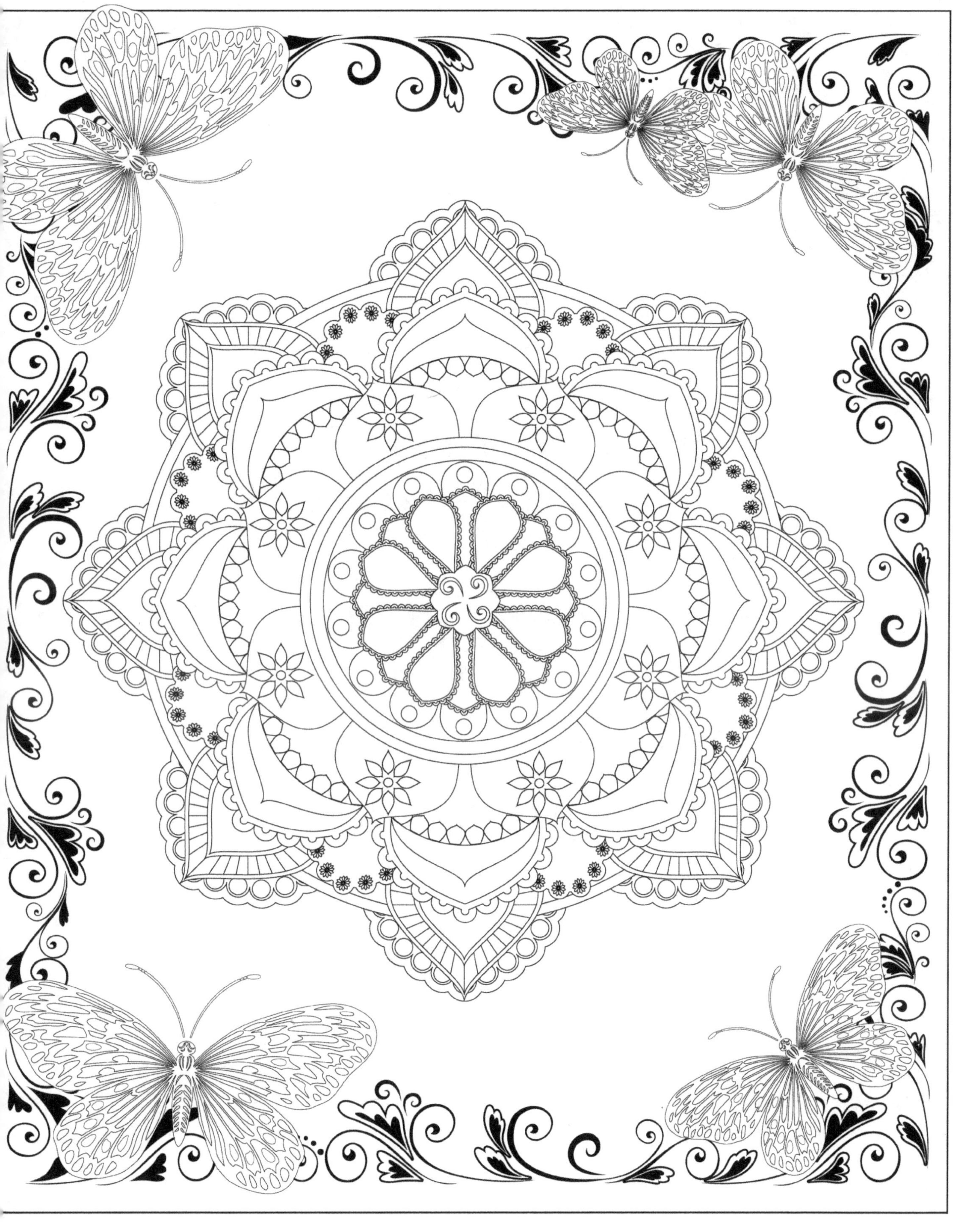

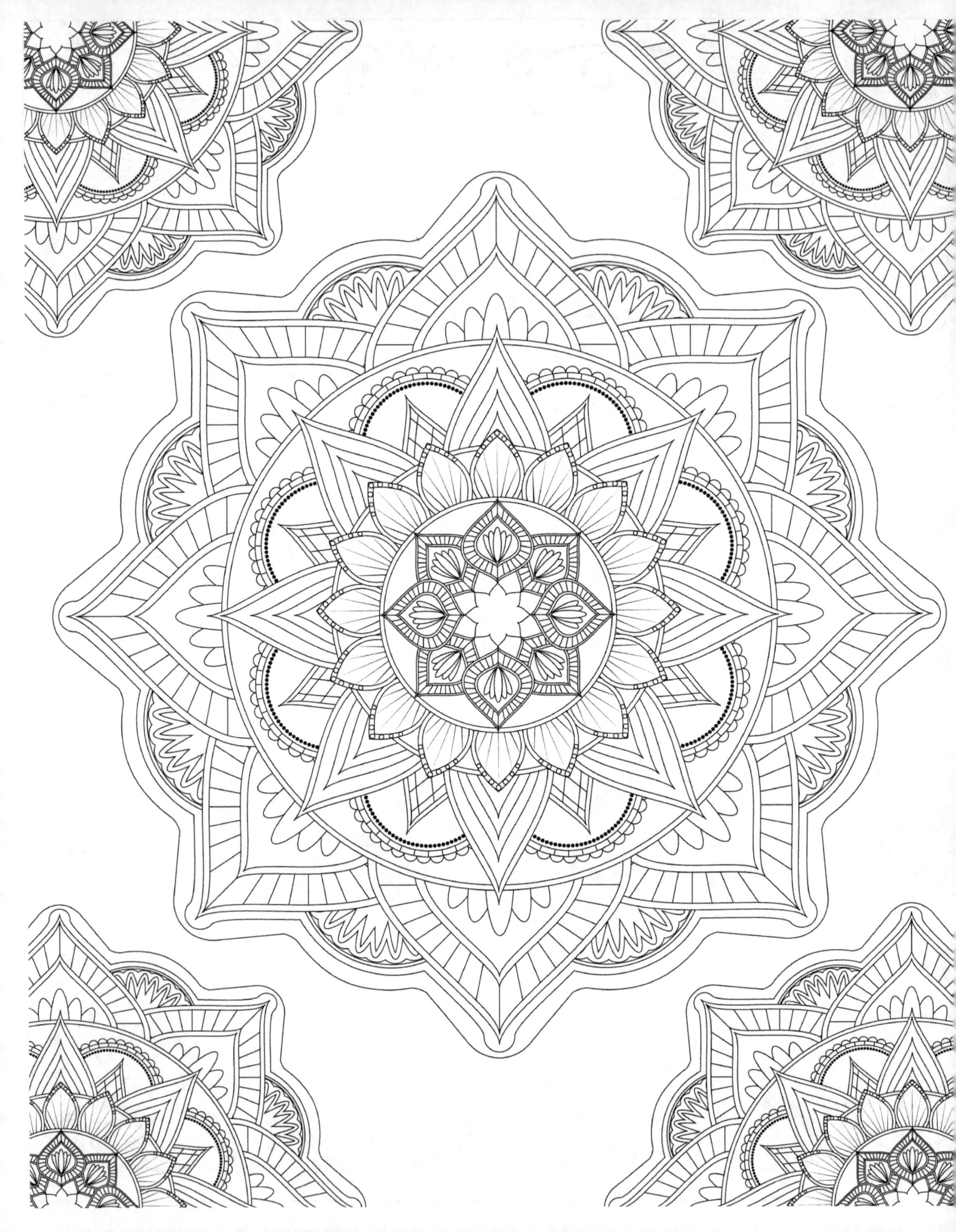

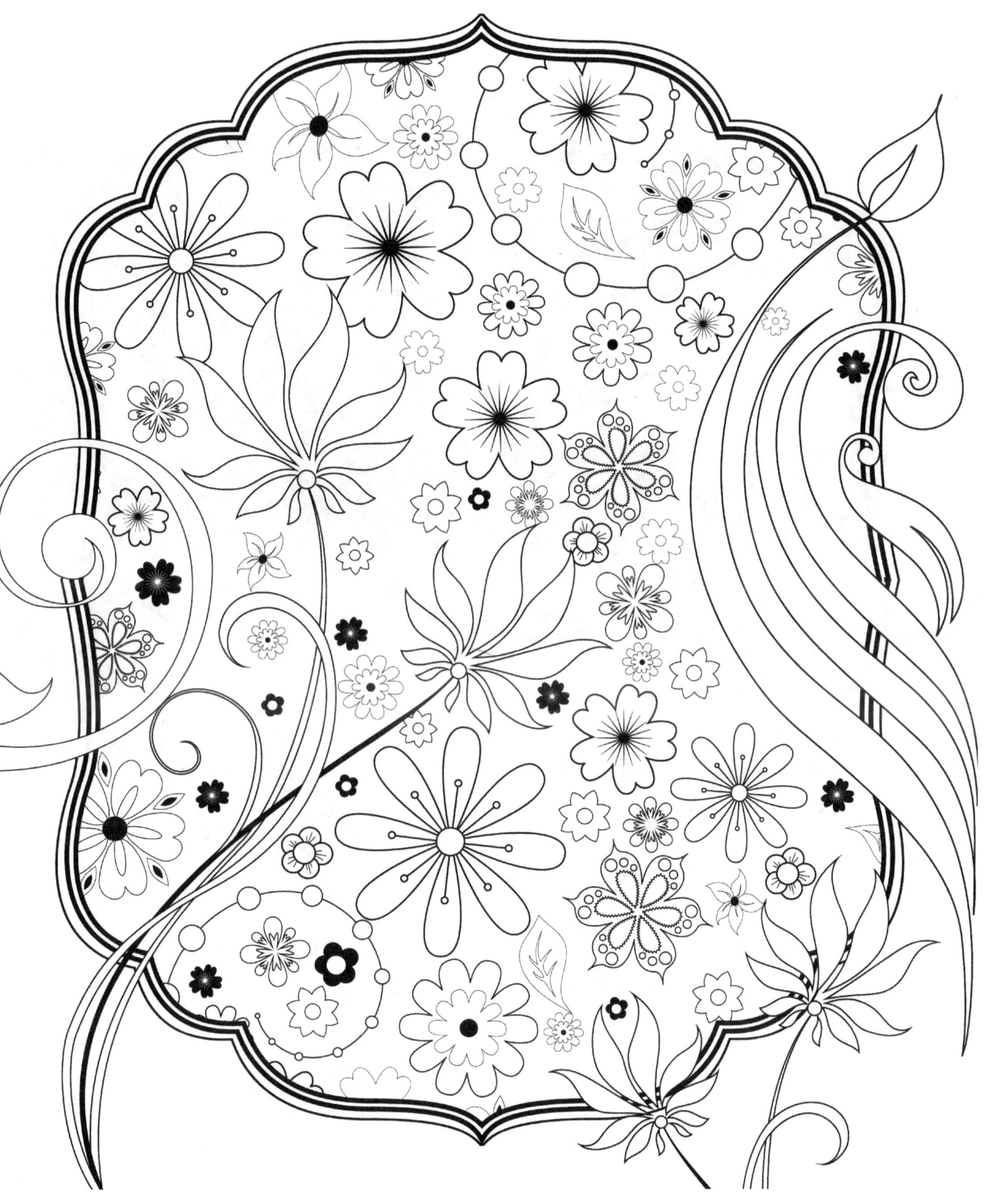

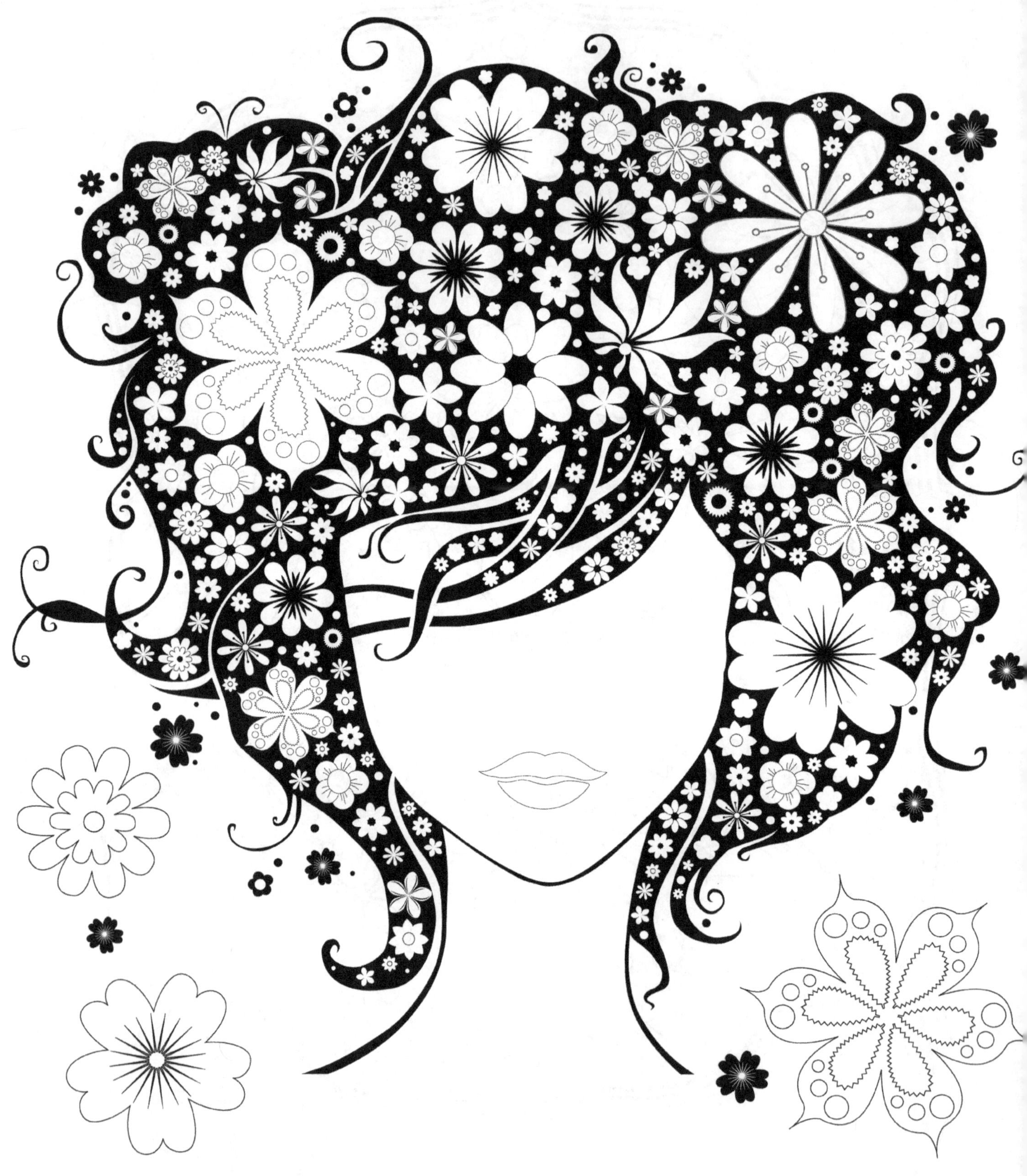

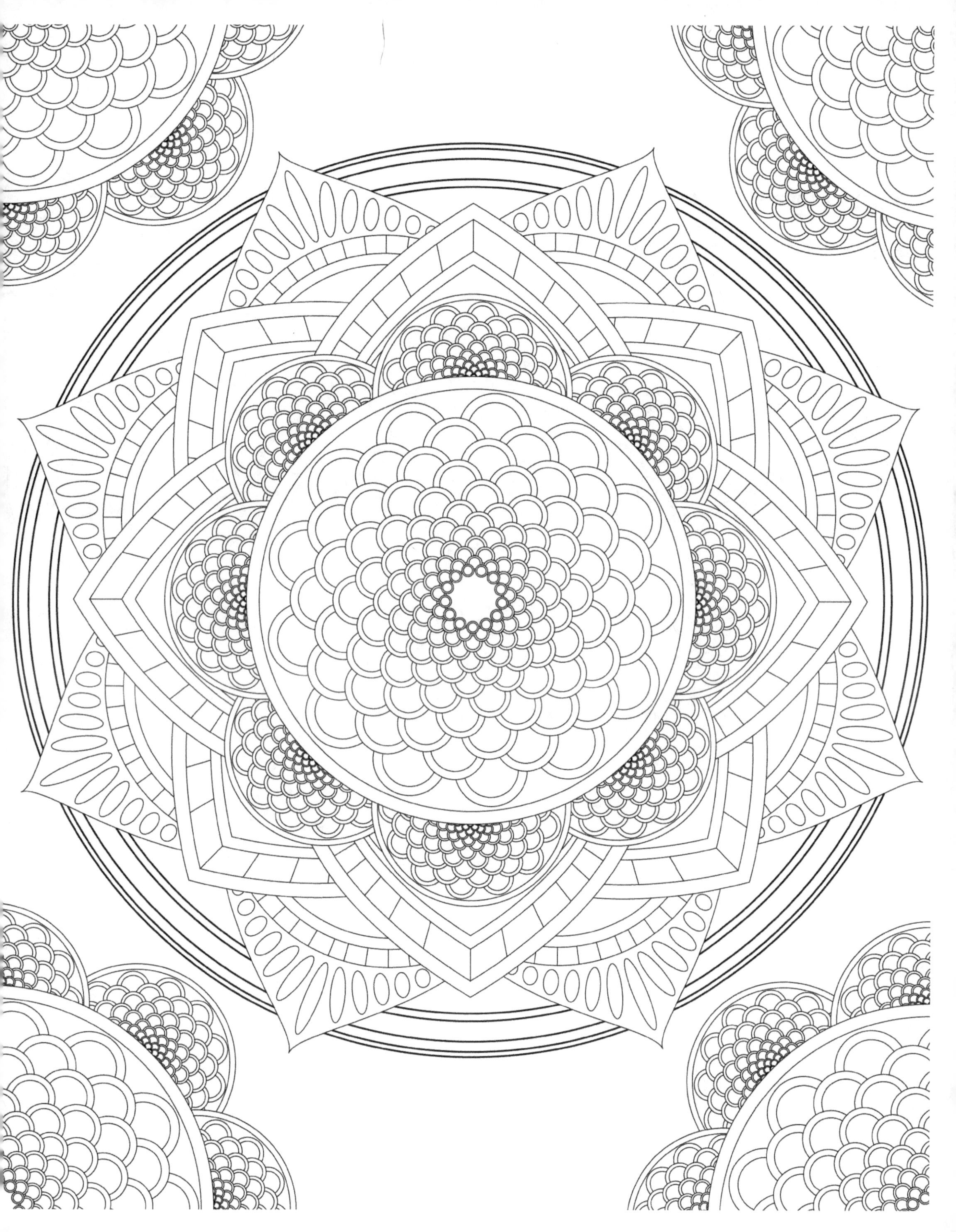

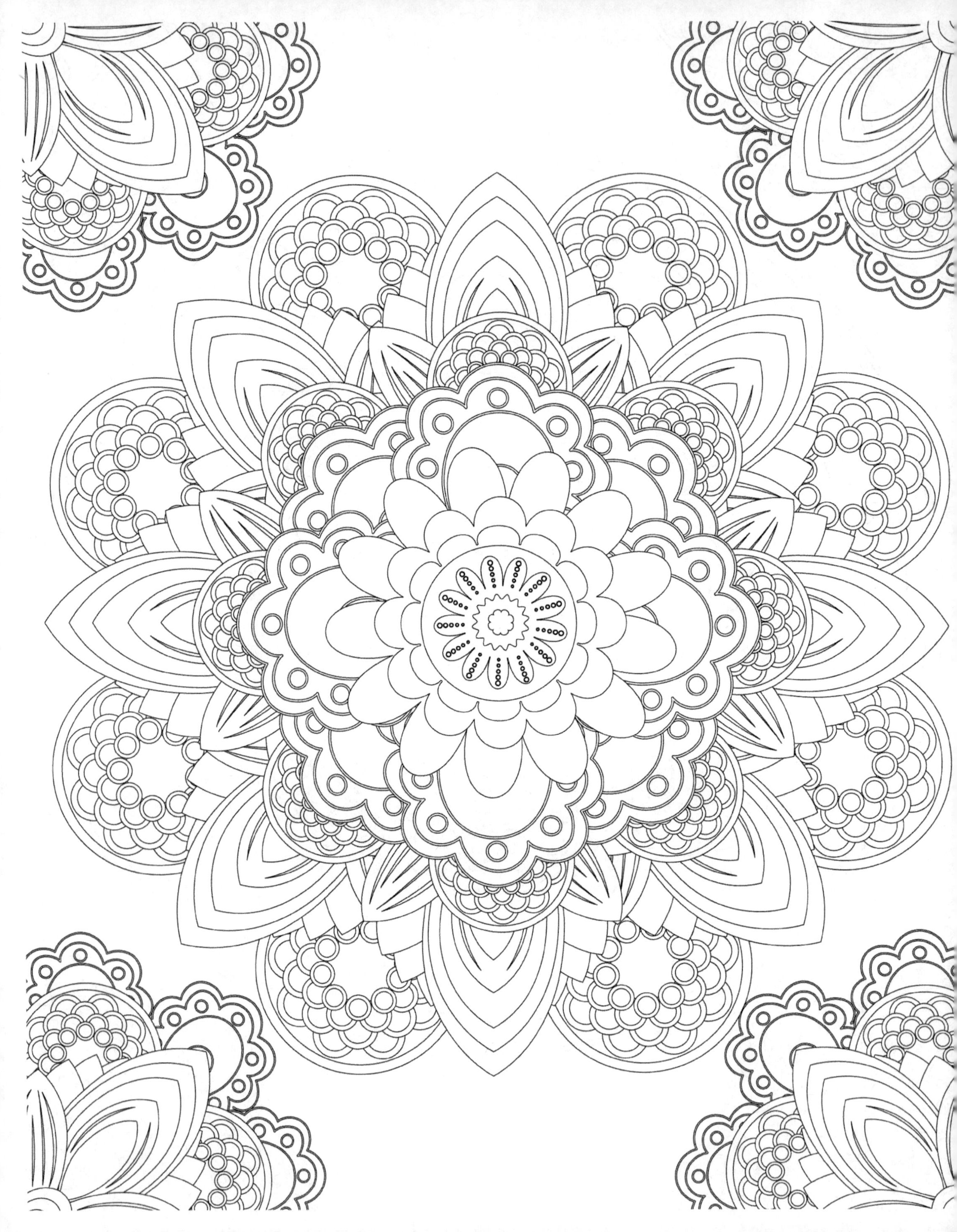

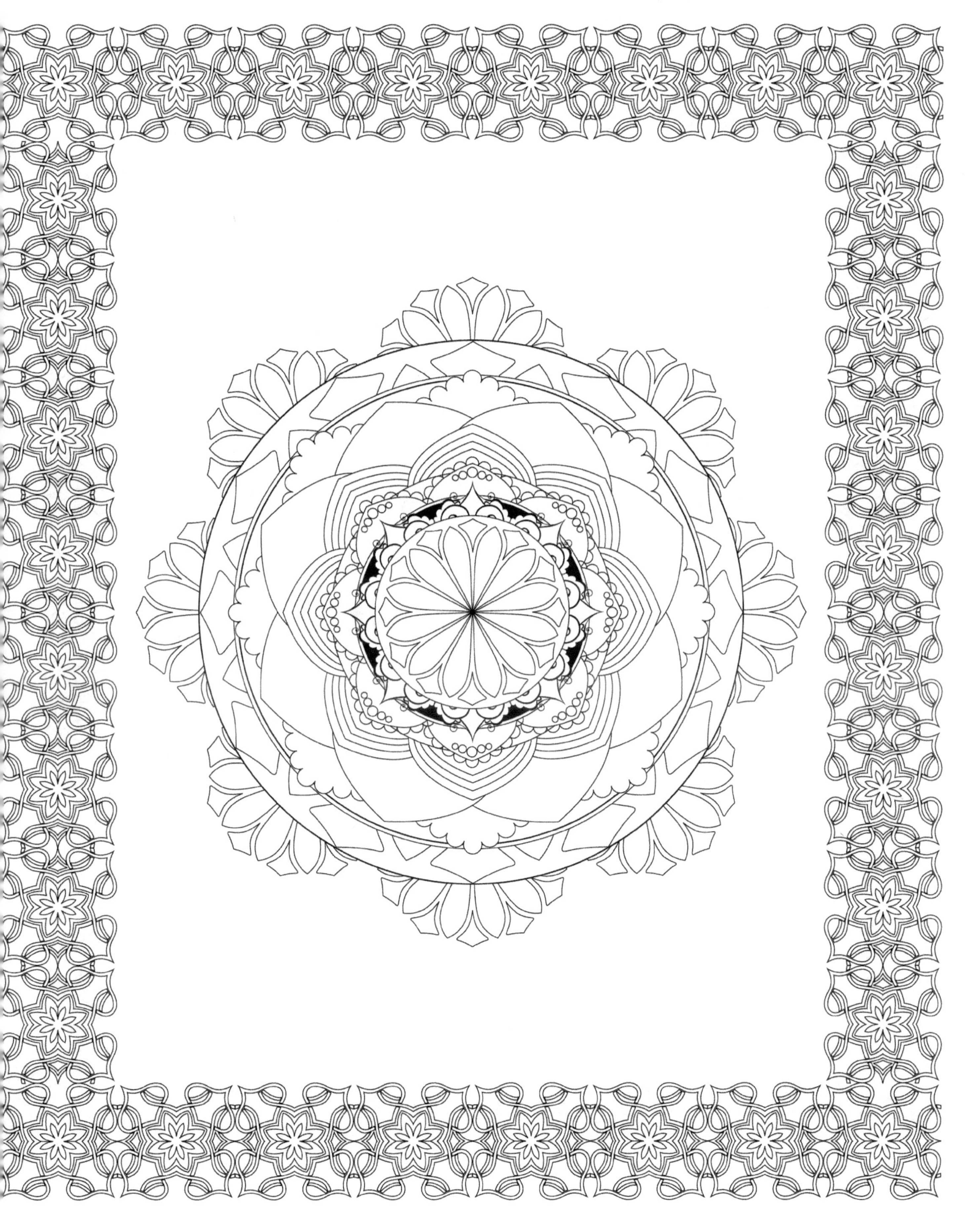

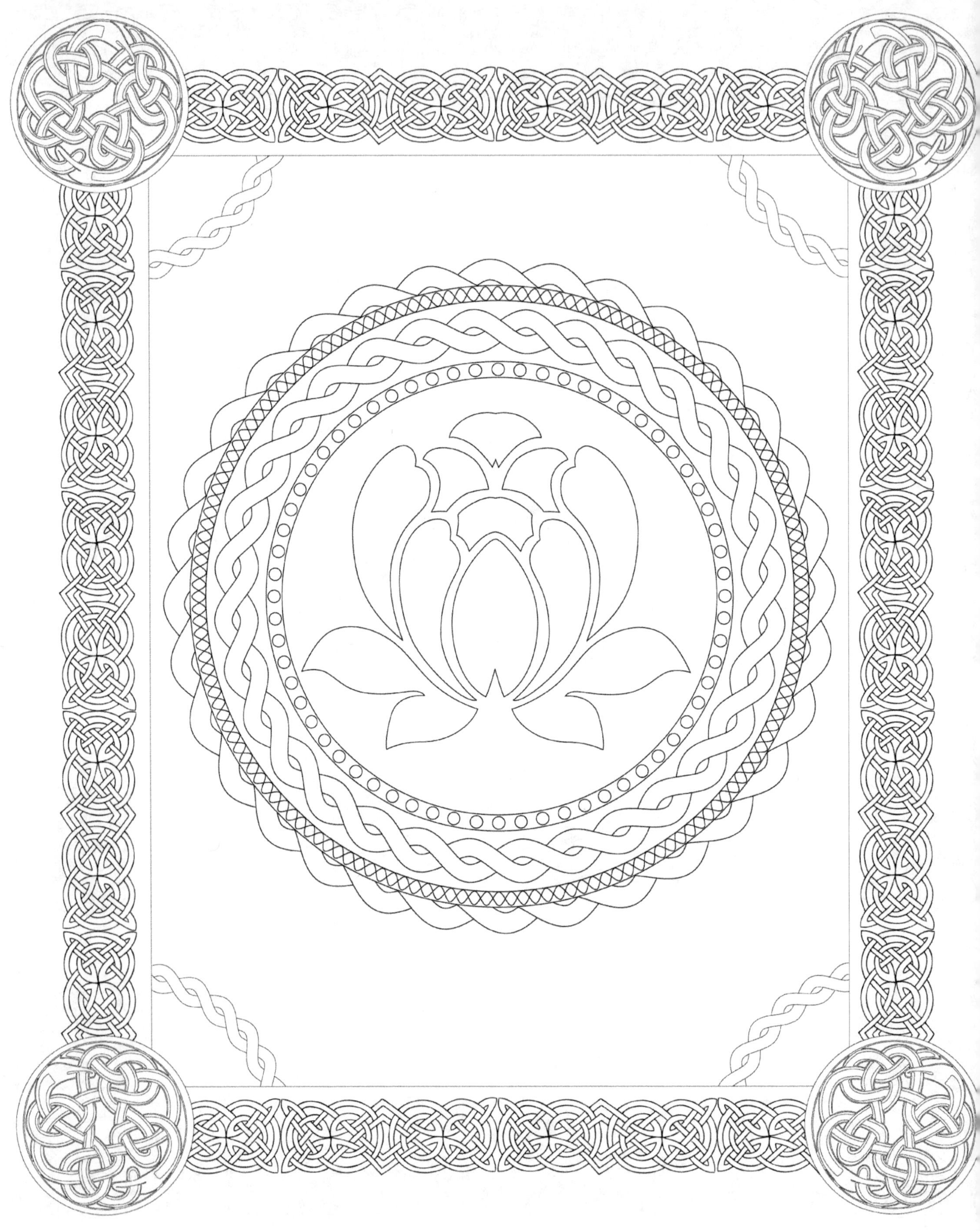

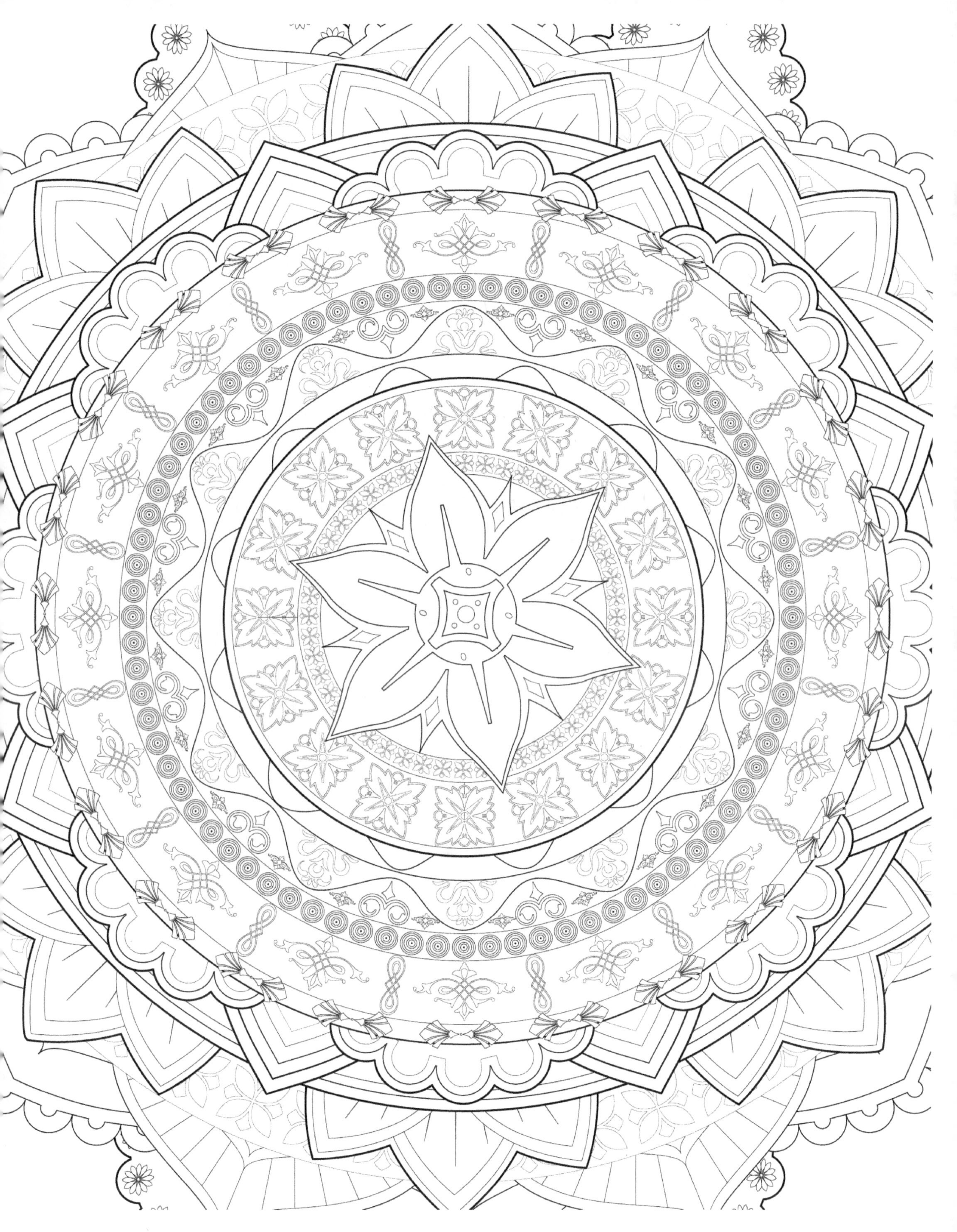

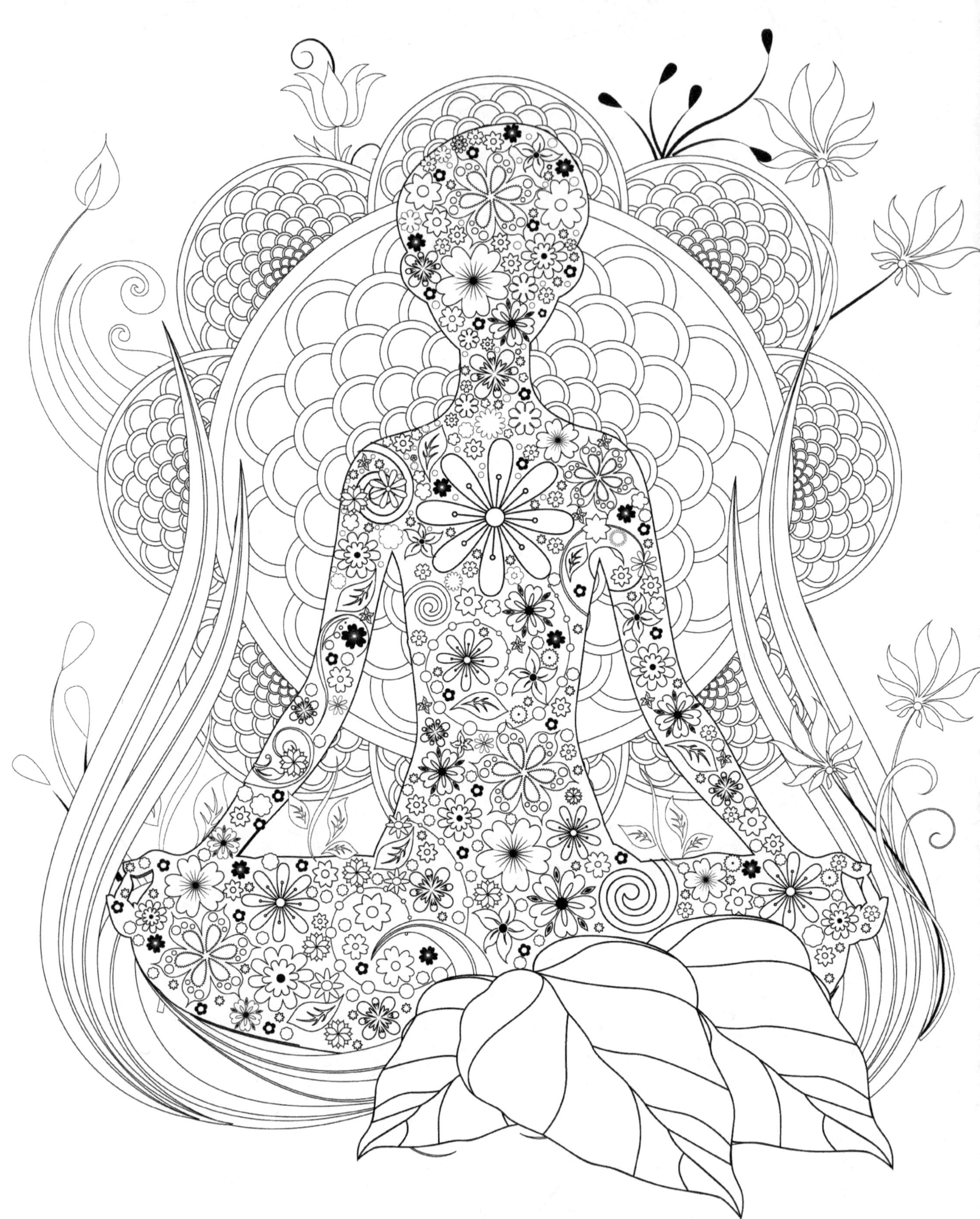

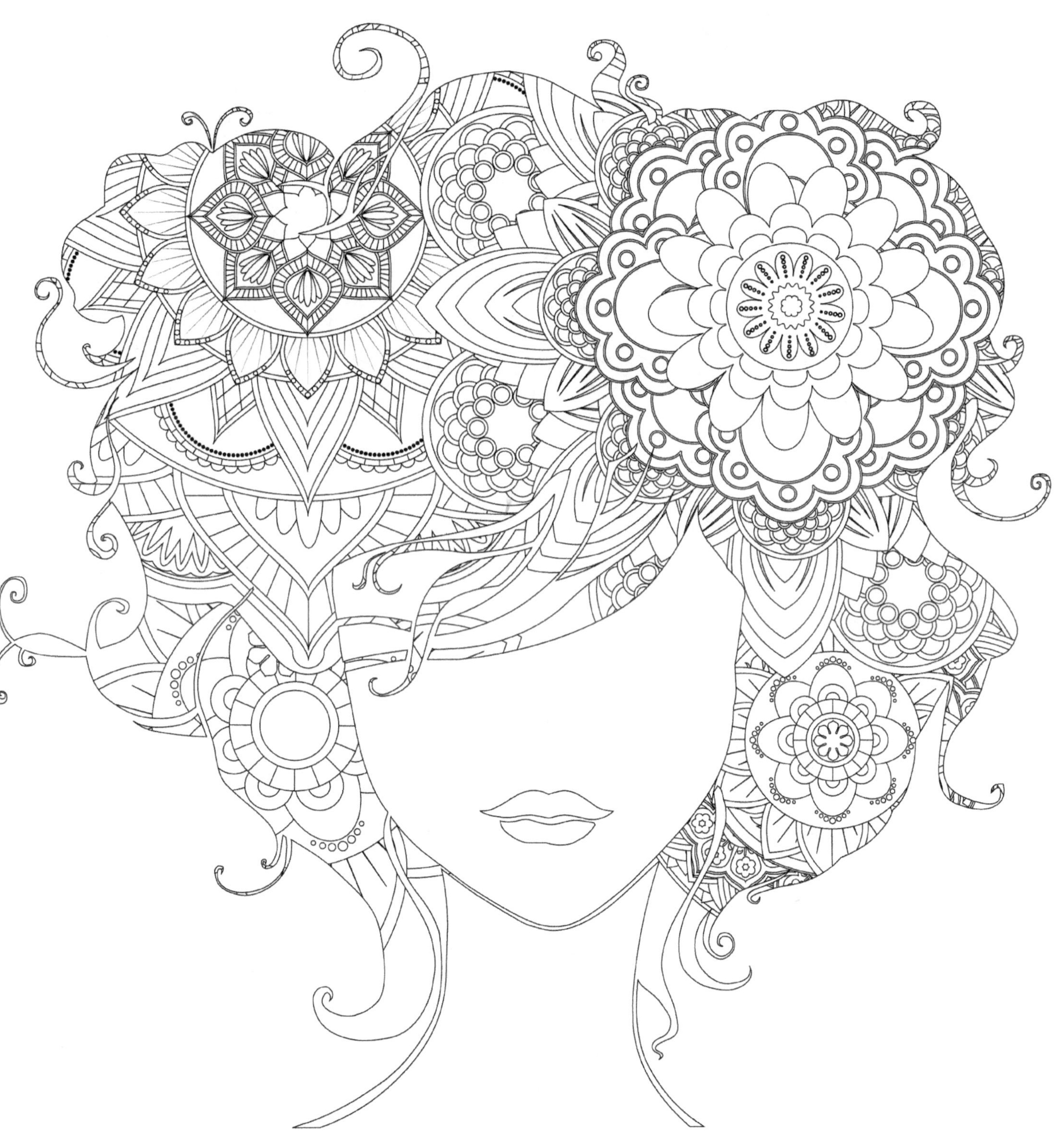

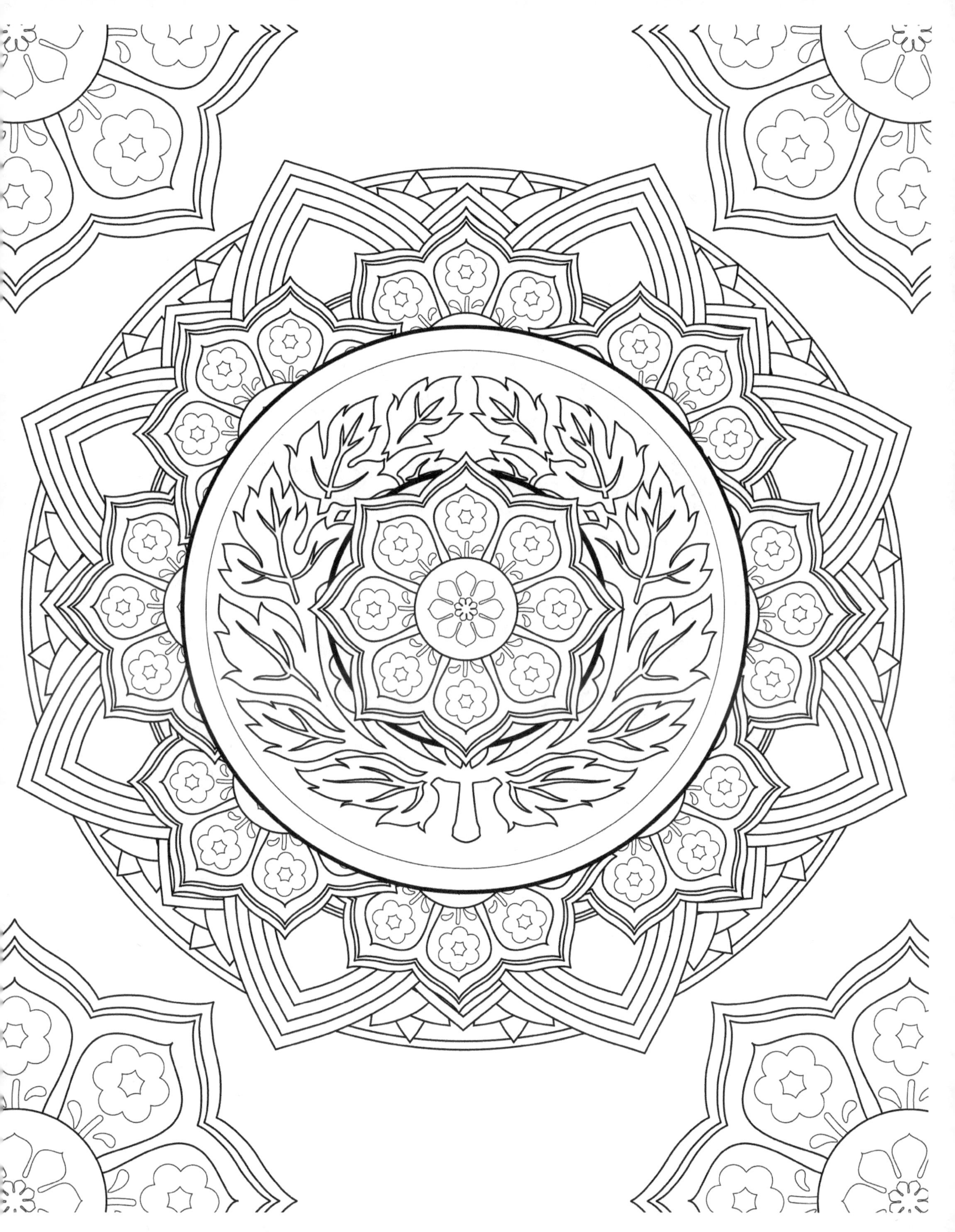

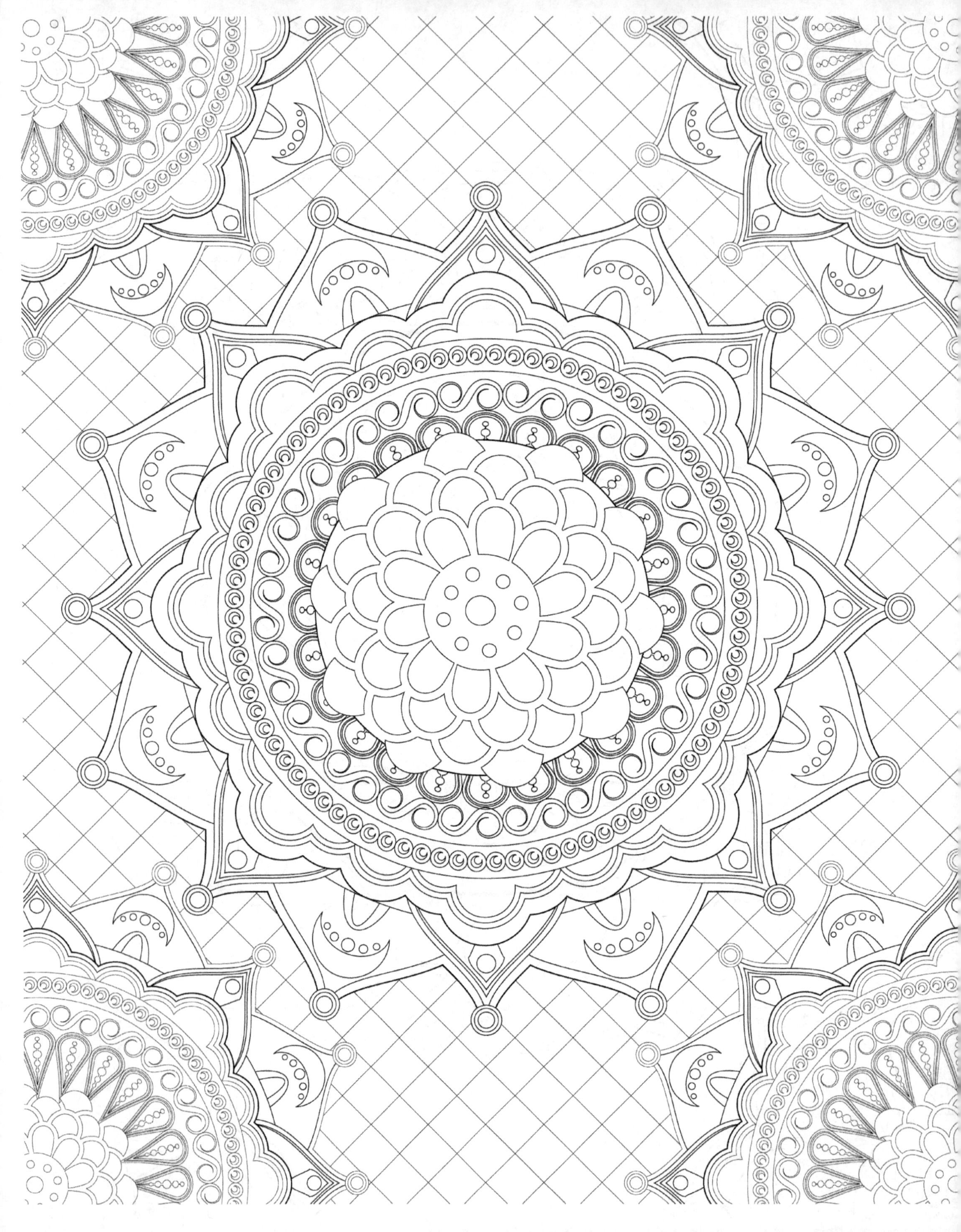

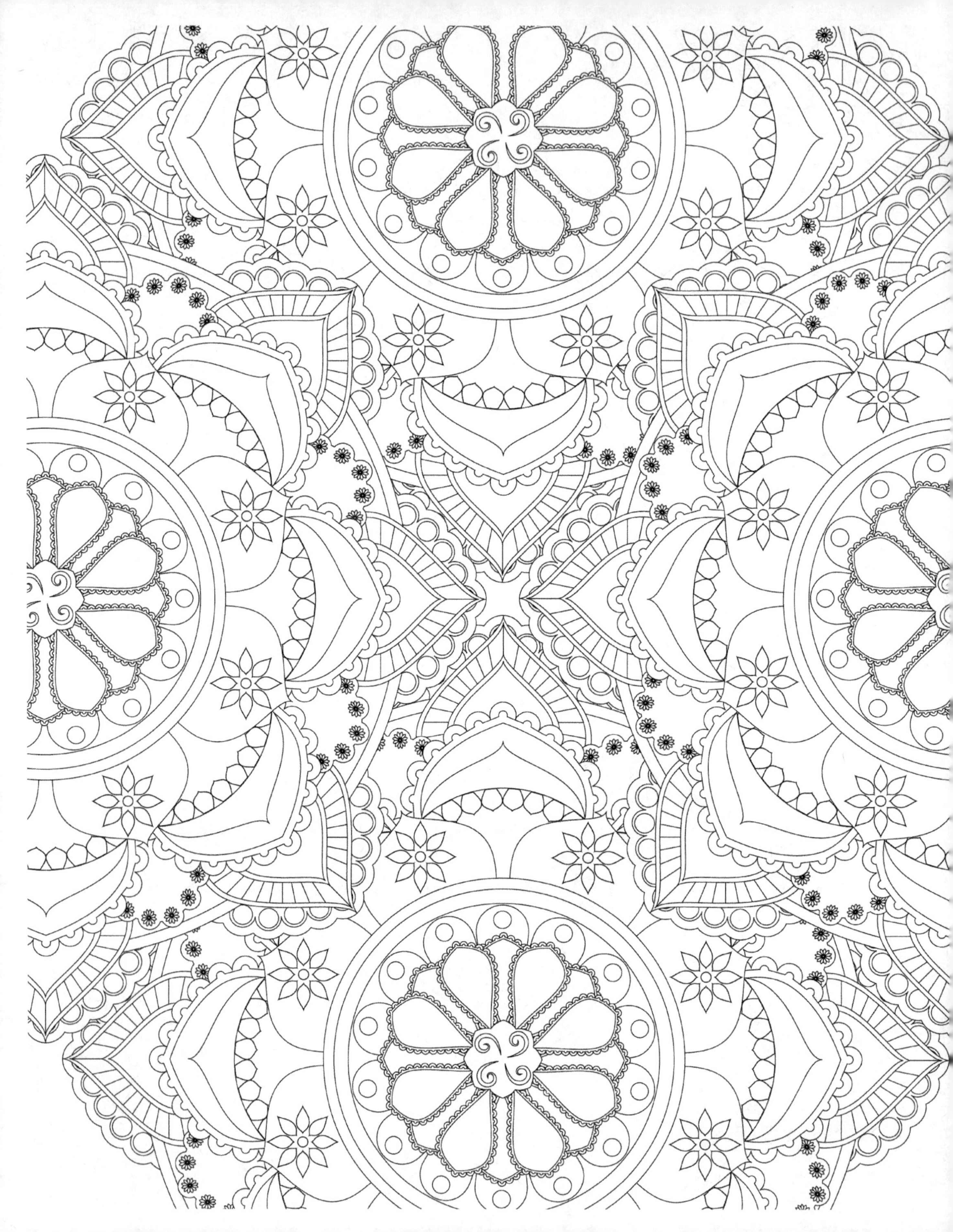

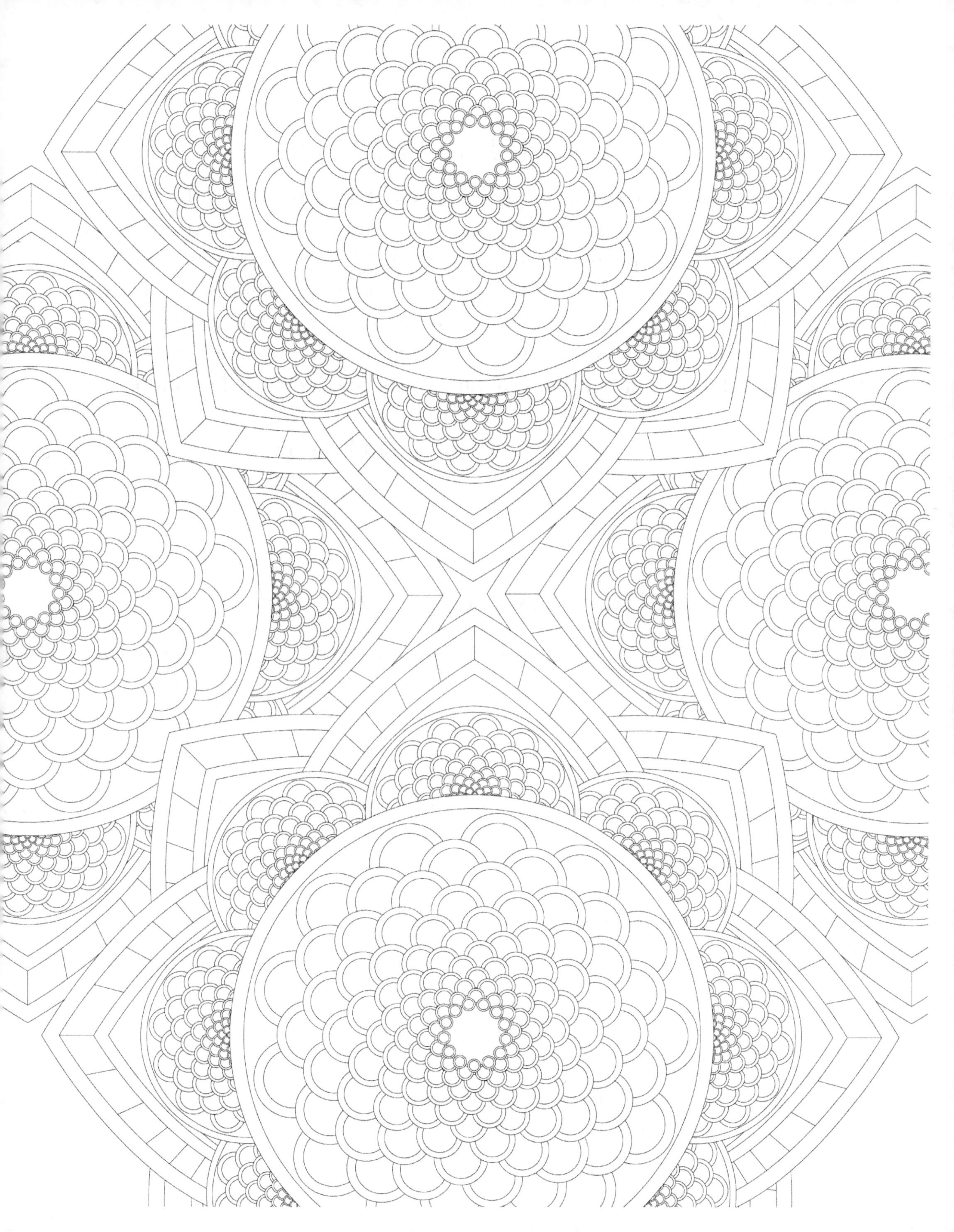

About The Author

Kiersten Fay was born with a set of crayons and an artist's soul. In school, art was her favorite elective, and that hasn't changed over the years, though it has manifested into different creative pursuits. She holds an Associate degree in Visual Communications, which led to a career in graphic design, but as it turned out, making up wild stories is her passion. Currently she is an accomplished romance author with two series' and seven full-length novels under her belt. She resides in Georgia with the love of her life, two quirky cats, and a clumsy but lovable dog.

Learn more at www.KierstenFay.com

Share Your Creations!

Once you start coloring, the page becomes your artistic expression, something unique to the world and we want to see it! Come to our Facebook page and share your creations with us.

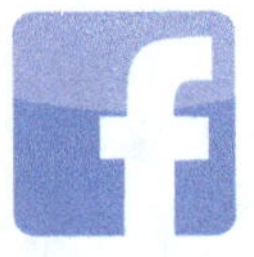

www.Facebook.com/AdultsColoringForFun

SERENITY: AN ADULT COLORING BOOK

ISBN-10: 0-9914197-5-8
ISBN-13: 978-0-9914197-5-3

www.ingramcontent.com/pod-product-compliance
Lightning Source LLC
La Vergne TN
LVHW081320110826
845149LV00006B/1552

* 9 7 8 0 9 9 1 4 1 9 7 5 3 *